GREAT

Stories & Songs

GREAT STORIES & SONGS

Leader's Resource Book – Code GS02

PO Box 288 Brookvale NSW 2100 Australia
Ph: (02) 9948 3957 Fax: (02) 9948 8153
Email: info@willowconnection.com.au
Website: www.willowconnection.com.au

This edition published in the United Kingdom by the Bible Reading Fellowship
First Floor, Elsfield Hall, 15-17 Elsfield Way, Oxford OX2 8FG, UK
Tel: 01865 319700 Fax: 01865 319701 Email: enquiries@brf.org.uk

ISBN 1 84101 251 3

First Published 2002
10 9 8 7 6 5 4 3 2 1 0

A catalogue record for this book is available from the British Library.

Project Manager and Concept: Monica O'Brien
Principal Writer: John O'Brien
Other Contributors: Mary Diggins, Anne Dohnt, Anne Christopher, Maria Millward and Monica O'Brien
Musical Compositions: Damien Halloran and Maria Millward
Cover Illustration: Peter Townsend
Editorial Assistance: Maria Millward
Design and Layout: Rod Heard
Music Typesetting: Graeme Evans

Other Resources: Compact Disc – Code GS01

Contents

Introduction, Notes and Rationale i

Aims ii

Layout and Structure ii

The Units at a Glance iii

Using this Resource iii

Using the Music iv

Unit 1 When We Listen 1

Unit 2 The Freedom to Choose 11

Unit 3 Gifts Freely Given 21

Unit 4 Bullies Big and Small 31

Unit 5 Riches in the Eyes of God 41

Unit 6 A Sense of the Sacred 53

Unit 7 Accepting Differences 63

Unit 8 When Things Go Wrong 73

Unit 9 Overcoming Fear 85

Unit 10 The Promise of New Life 97

Music Scores 108

Overhead Transparency Masters 136

Introduction

Great Stories & Songs is a contemporary Christian resource providing original stories, songs, creative group and individual activities, scripture, prayers and rituals which explore a range of issues and themes that are relevant to children 8-12 years of age. (Grades 3-7)

Great Stories & Songs includes:

1. Leader's Book

Arranged in ten units, the book contains an introduction to each unit of work, learning outcomes for each unit, ten contemporary stories, a selection of age-appropriate group and individual activities, biblical references, discussion starters, prayers, music scores, overhead transparency masters and lyrics for songs specially written to accompany the written materials.

2. Music Recording

The Compact Disc presents ten professionally recorded original songs featuring lead vocals by adults and children and backing vocals by a children's choir. It also offers complete backing tracks for each song.

Notes

The Bible references quoted within this book are taken from the popular 'Contemporary English Version,' which is widely used with children.

Rationale

Great Stories & Songs assists children in developing a wide range of skills, knowledge, values and attitudes associated with being a follower of Jesus. It provides a basis for ongoing reflection and action as Christians responding to life's many blessings and challenges. Great Stories & Songs seeks to foster in children a deeper faith, encouraging them to develop a closer relationship with God and all people.

Aims

Great Stories & Songs aims to:

- be child-centred.
- foster a spiritual foundation which integrates life and faith.
- provide an accessible, 'user friendly' teaching/ministry resource for adults.
- explore relevant, age-appropriate issues and themes that support the principles and outcomes of a broad section of Christian Education curriculums throughout Australia and beyond.
- be ecumenical.
- offer a contemporary, interactive format.

Layout and Structure

Each unit in the Great Stories & Songs Leader's Book is arranged in an easy to follow format. The sections in each unit include:

- Overview (introducing the Unit and providing background information for the leader)
- Outcomes (assisting the leader with planning)
- Getting Started (introducing the children to the theme and story)
- The Story
- Sharing (providing thought-provoking questions to stimulate group interaction)
- Activities (suggesting a minimum of three individual or group activities)
- Scripture (situating the theme within the context of God's Word)
- Prayer (providing an experience of prayer)
- Song (providing contemporary musical arrangements and thought-provoking lyrics)
- Action (suggesting a personal response)

Full music scores and overhead transparency masters are also provided in the back of the book.

The Units at a Glance

A variety of themes and issues that are relevant to children 8-12 years of age are explored in Great Stories & Songs. The following table outlines the theme, the story, the song and the symbols used.

Unit	Theme	Story	Song	Symbol
1	When We Listen	Tales	When We Listen	Own symbols
2	The Freedom to Choose	Puppet	We've Got the Power	Puppets
3	Gifts Freely Given	Rag Doll	Good Things	Post & Gift Box
4	Bullies Big and Small	Joining the Library	We Will Bring Your Peace	Bubbles
5	Riches in the Eyes of God	The Fire-Dragon	I Will Bless You, Lord	Water
6	A Sense of the Sacred	Piper in the Sand	Welcome to God's House	Various items
7	Accepting Differences	Creature From the Stars	Do to Others	Shoes
8	When Things Go Wrong	Apples	Happy Are All of My Children	Seeds
9	Overcoming Fear	The Staircase	We will Make a Place Ready	–
10	The Promise of New Life	The Empty Desk	Nothing Can Take Us Away	Butterfly

Using this Resource

This resource is designed to be used by both experienced group leaders, and those who have just begun the role. It recognizes that people who lead groups possess varying degrees of knowledge and experience. In light of this, the authors encourage you, as a leader using this book, to draw on your own creativity in order to bring the content to life. Much of the content lends itself to further development and this is welcomed.

We suggest you look for opportunities to expand the use of the material by tapping into your creativity and the creativity of the children. You may, for example, wish to include props when telling and re-telling the stories. The story *Puppet*, in the unit titled *The Freedom to Choose*, lends itself to the use of a range of puppets and circus figures. The children themselves could be invited to re-tell the story using these props chosen or created by them.

The prayer times are designed to lead the children into a deeper relationship with God. Not all children are comfortable with shared prayer, silence or the use of prayer responses. In these cases, you are encouraged to adapt the content to facilitate the prayer experience. Leading by example is often the least threatening way to introduce the children to a new or different style of prayer. Any methods or tools that enrich these special times are encouraged.

Using the Music

One of the most valuable aspects of this resource is the inclusion of original, contemporary music which compliments and expands upon the themes explored in the various units.

The music accompaniments within this book have been arranged in an accessible form for keyboard, guitar and selected instruments. It is important to be aware that these musical arrangements may differ from the recorded arrangements used on the Great Stories & Songs Compact Disc which features lead vocals by both adults and children, a children's backing choir and instrumental backing tracks for each song.

When We Listen

Unit 1

Overview

From the typical child's perspective, the world is full of people who expect them to listen. Parents, teachers, relatives and pastors all have plenty to say at times, and all expect kids to take on board the messages, dictates, rules and guidelines articulated.

Sadly, those of us who expect children to listen do not always prove to be good listeners ourselves. We are often too busy, too tired or too preoccupied to always listen to children at what might be highly inconvenient moments. This rather hypocritical situation does not really offer children a good example.

Listening is important. Effective communication cannot take place without the essential ingredient: listening. We want children to listen effectively - to their friends, to parents, to teachers and to God. Ideally, they should be confident that others - friends, parents, teachers and God - will listen to them, too.

This unit focuses on both aspects of this theme. In the story ***Tales***, a boy realises his mother is not really listening to him, and he spins an outrageous yarn in the hope of getting her attention. The reflection and prayer focus on listening to God.

Outcomes

The children will:

- **understand that listening is a vital form of effective communication.**
- **identify their own listening habits and those of the people around them.**
- **recognise that God is a great listener.**
- **understand that if they listen patiently, they will hear God speaking to them through silence, the events of their daily lives, through people, nature and through God's Word.**

Getting Started

Explain to the children that they are going to explore the theme of listening. The following questions and comments may serve as an introduction to the theme and the story.

Do you ever find that people don't listen to you? Listening is important but often we don't focus on what people are telling us, and sometimes those who expect us to listen don't seem so interested in what we have to say.

The world would be a better place if we all listened with a sympathetic ear - to our friends, our families and to God. We would all understand each other much better.

In the following story, ***Tales***, a boy finds that his mother is not really listening - yet again. He begins to tell her the most unusual story, in the hope that she will focus on him.

Story

Tales by John O'Brien

When Andrew got home from school, he found Mum reading a book.

"Hello, Mum," he said.

"Hello, Andrew," said Mum. "Had a good day?" She picked up her coffee, and sipped at it. And she read her book some more.

"No," said Andrew. "I had a bad day. You see, Jason spilt some paint on the floor and he told Miss Connors that I did it. She wouldn't believe me when I said that I didn't. She made me clean it all up."

"That's nice, dear," said Mum. She flipped a page of her book. "That's lovely."

Andrew sighed. It was always the same. Mum never listened to him properly. Never!

"Something else happened," he said, smiling just a little. "It happened on the way home from school."

"I see," said Mum, sipping her coffee again.

"There was this elephant lying on the pavement, and when I tried to get past, it grabbed me with its trunk and threw me out on the road. And a truck ran over me, squashing me flat. Blood went everywhere!"

"That's good, dear," Mum murmured.

"Then a lady in a pink car stopped right beside me," Andrew went on. "She opened the boot of her car, and a monkey jumped out. It was a magic monkey - all white, with little black eyes - and it waved a magic wand over me, and suddenly I was all right."

Mum nodded a little, and read more of her book. Andrew thought for a moment.

"And later, Mum, another car stopped beside me. There was a horrible man inside. 'Get into my car, little boy!' he screamed. 'Get in and I'll give you some chocolate!' So I did get in, even though I shouldn't have." Andrew stopped for a moment, staring at Mum. "Well, Mum, what do you think of that?"

"Very nice, dear," murmured Mum. "It sounds like you had a lovely day." And she kept reading.

"The man drove away ever so fast," Andrew told her. "And all of a sudden, I noticed that there were bones on the floor of his car. People bones! Just about my size, too! I felt really scared. I felt that terrible things were about to happen. But I was lucky, because the man had run out of chocolate, and when he stopped to get some, I ran away."

"I see," Mum said softly.

Andrew scratched his head. "Then this space ship came shooting down from the sky. It landed right by me, and a blue alien with two heads jumped out. It pointed this funny gun at me and shot me. And when I got hit, I turned green and grew six arms. That's why I look all funny this afternoon."

"Oh," said Mum. She didn't even bother to look up at him.

Andrew sighed. It was no good. Mum simply wasn't going to listen.

"I'm going out to play with Paul," he said, and went off to put on some old clothes.

"Bye!" he called out, a few minutes later. "I'm going now!"

"Where are you going?" Mum called out.

"Oh, Mum," said Andrew, hurrying into the room once more. "I'm going to play with Paul! I told you so a minute ago!"

"With Paul?" said Mum, looking up from her book. "Well, just make sure you don't start behaving like him. I was talking to his mother this morning, and she says he tells the most terrible tales!"

"Oh, Mum," said Andrew, starting to go. "Paul's all right."

"And not only that," Mum called after him. "But I was told that he never listens to a thing anyone tells him. Never! And I won't have anyone like that in this house! Understand?"

Andrew smiled to himself as he went. "Sure, Mum," he said, "I understand."

Sharing

When did Andrew first realise that Mum wasn't listening to him again?

How do you think he felt when he realised that she wasn't listening to him? Why?

He makes up a really strange tale, trying to get her attention. If she had been listening, how do you think she would have reacted to some of the things he told her? Why?

What problems could Mum's poor listening cause for Andrew in the future?

Can you think of people who haven't listened very well to you at times?

How do you feel when people don't listen?

Are there times when you don't listen as well as you might? How do you feel about this? Why do you think you should make an effort to listen well?

Scripture

Jesus was a good listener. He always gave attention to those who needed it. He always focused on what people were saying. One day, to their surprise, his disciples found this out.

Jesus and his disciples went to his home in Capernaum. After they were inside the house, Jesus asked them, "What were you arguing about along the way?"
They had been arguing about which one of them was the greatest, and so they didn't answer.
After Jesus sat down and told the twelve disciples to gather around

him, he said, "If you want the place of honour, you must become as a slave and serve others." (Mark 9: 33-35)

How can we tell from this passage that Jesus was a good listener?

As well as hearing the argument, Jesus has clearly thought about it. He has used it to present a powerful teaching to the disciples. What is this teaching?

How might Jesus want us to listen to others? Why?

Activities

1. When People Don't Listen

Discuss with the children situations they've experienced when people haven't listened to them (e.g. a teacher not listening to a student, a parent not having time to listen to a problem or difficulty).

Ask how things might have been better if the person had listened patiently.

Divide the group into threes and ask them to develop short role-plays in which one of them will be trying to explain about a problem they've encountered. The first person they talk to won't be a good listener, and the problem won't be resolved. The second person they speak to will be a patient and thoughtful listener who will help to solve the problem.

The following suggestions for the role-plays may be useful.

Going to see someone about:

- loud noise neighbours are making late one night
- a brand new computer that is not working
- incorrect plane tickets that were sent home by a travel agent
- a faulty appliance that a plumber or electrician did not fix properly
- a robbery that the police have forgotten to investigate

After a short preparation time, the children present the plays to the class and discuss.

2. Listening to God

Talk with the group about ways God might try to speak to us.

Draw up a list, such as: through

- scripture
- our consciences
- other people
- song
- prayer
- quiet reflection
- creation

Discuss how our world would be different and better if everyone really listened to God.

Draw up a list of the children's responses such as:

- less crime
- less violence
- more caring
- less poverty
- more generosity

On a large sheet of paper or cardboard, draw up a heading: 'A World That Listens to God'

Have the children draw and colour pictures that help illustrate this, then paste or stick them to the large sheet. This sheet can be used as a focus for prayer.

3. Radio Plays

For this activity you will need a tape recorder and a cassette tape.

Explain to the group that everyone is going to make up short radio plays relating to an incident in the life of Jesus. The incidents used should be ones that the students remember well. Explain that they are to tell the whole story using just voices and sound effects.

Suggest some possibilities such as:

- a well-known miracle
- Jesus travelling with his disciples
- an incident in the temple

Divide the children into small groups for discussion, practice and recording.

Later, share the results and discuss.

Prayer

Ask the children to bring their work, 'A World That Listens to God', to the prayer time. Hang or position the work in a visible place where the children meet for the prayer. Children may also bring other items which, for them, symbolise listening to God, e.g. open Bible, candle etc., and use these to set up the sacred space.

When it is time to begin, ask the children to sit in a circle and make sure they are comfortable. Explain to them that during the reflection there will be short pauses for them to think and pray quietly.

Place a plastic bowl of water and about six small stones in the centre of the circle. Tell the children that some small stones will be dropped into the bowl. Ask them to listen quietly and to prepare themselves for prayer. Slowly and prayerfully drop each stone into the bowl of water.

The following reflection is read.

Make yourself as comfortable as you can.
Close your eyes.
Take a deep breath and breathe out slowly.
Try to relax. Relax your arms, your legs.
Relax every muscle.

Listen.
Listen to the sounds around you...
(Pause)
Listen to the clearest sounds, the closest sounds you can hear.
What are they?
(Pause)
Now listen to sounds more distant. The softest sounds you can hear.
The quietest.
(Pause)

We normally block out many sounds.
Much of the noise around us we don't really hear.
Life is often too fast and hectic.
Some days there is no time to listen at all.
(Pause)

Do we sometimes fail to listen to God?
God speaks to us in many ways.
But the voice of God is a quiet, gentle voice.
A voice that is easily lost in the rush of life.
Do we make time to listen to God?
(Pause)

We can hear God through our inner voice, through our conscience.
But do we listen?
(Pause)
We can hear God through scripture and through prayer.
But do we listen?
(Pause)
We can hear the voice of God through the calm and peaceful sounds of nature, the sounds of creation.
But do we listen?
(Pause)

The children are invited to pray the following prayer together.

Jesus, our friend,
So often we find little time to listen to you.
Help us to find that time.
Help us to find the space, the quiet and the patience needed to hear the voice of your Holy Spirit.
Your voice is soft and gentle, unlike the loud, harsh sounds that fill our world.
You use it to speak to us in so many ways.
If only we would find the time to listen, we would come to understand your wishes, hopes and dreams for us.
Help us to listen to you always. Amen.

Invite the children to join in singing, ***When We Listen***.

Song

Unit 1

When We Listen

Damien Halloran & Maria Millward

When we listen, we will hear you,
In the towering voices of mountains and seas.
When we listen, we will hear you,
In the gentlest song of the breeze.

Chorus:

When we listen, we will hear you,
Speaking to us of your wonderful ways.
When we listen, we will hear you,
Guiding us all of our days.

When we listen, we will hear you,
In the welcoming warmth of our fam'ly and friends.
When we listen, we will hear you,
In the laughter and love that you send.

Chorus

When we listen, we will hear you,
In the stories and songs that your people have heard.
When we listen, we will hear you,
In the power of your holy word.

Chorus

Action

Today, I will make a conscious effort to listen attentively to my parents, friends, neighbours and to God.

The Freedom to Choose

Unit 2

Overview

Pain and suffering are experienced by all who travel through life, though not in equal measure. Some of us are fortunate enough to be touched by tragedy only occasionally, while others, often at a young age, are endlessly tormented by anguish, fear or pain.

How is it that an all-powerful, all-loving God can allow pain and suffering to strike at the innocent in such a random fashion? This question is one of the most challenging that theologians have had to grapple with over the past two thousand years. Today it continues to puzzle many, although a part of the answer is clear. It relates to our own personal freedom - and it is the focus of this unit.

We are all free to act as we choose; this is a part of what makes us human. We can choose, if we want, to hurt those around us in any number of ways, and God, in a sense, is powerless to prevent this hurt. If God did prevent it, we would be little more than puppets, controlled by celestial strings, dancing to a heavenly tune, without any hint of free will at all.

In the following story, a puppet is forced by a cruel ringmaster to take part in several painful acts. The discussion and reflection following the story is designed to encourage children to see that God must allow pain and suffering if we are to remain free, unlike puppets, who are forced to dance to the tunes of others.

Outcomes

The children will:

- **recognise that they are free to make just and unjust choices.**
- **understand that God, by loving them unconditionally, shows them how to treat others well and to make good choices.**
- **identify that much of the pain and suffering found in the world is a result of human greed and cruelty.**

Getting Started

There is a lot of sadness, pain and suffering in our world. We all feel these things at times. Sadly, sometimes our hurt is caused by those around us.

People can be cruel and selfish. All of us can be mean to others - and all of us are mean at times. We don't have to be, but we are. God's hope is that we will treat each other well, but God will not make us do so. God has given us the freedom to choose and this freedom will never be taken away.

The following story is about a puppet who is forced to do several unpleasant things. Like all puppets, he is not able to choose what he will do. He hasn't been given the wonderful gift of freedom like us, and he has to take desperate measures to get it.

Story

Puppet by John O'Brien

"Where is Puppet?" demanded Ringmaster. "I want him to dance in the fire. The crowds will love that for sure!"

"But won't Puppet burn his legs if he dances in the fire?" asked Juggler.

"That won't matter!" cried Ringmaster. "It will be a great sight to see - Puppet dancing in the fire! People will pay a lot of money to see him dancing in the flames! I'll be rich!"

"Well, I don't know where he is," said Juggler, as he sharpened his juggling knives for the evening show. "Maybe Lion Tamer has seen him."

Ringmaster hurried through the circus, towards the lion cages. "Lion Tamer!" he yelled. "I'm looking for Puppet! Do you know where he is?"

Lion Tamer shook his enormous bushy head of hair. "I haven't seen Puppet all day," he said. "Maybe he's hiding. He gets frightened sometimes, you know."

"Why should Puppet get frightened?" asked Ringmaster.

"Because of the things you make him do," explained Lion Tamer. "You made him dance with my lions last night and he got badly scratched!"

"I was only trying to make a bit of money," explained Ringmaster.

"Anyway, he doesn't have to dance with the lions tonight. I want him to dance in the fire instead!"

"In the fire?" cried the Lion Tamer.

"Sure!" cried Ringmaster. "People will love it! They'll pay plenty to see Puppet dance in the fire!"

"But it'll hurt him," whispered Lion Tamer. "It really will."

"What would you know?" asked Ringmaster. "I'm going to see Wire Walker. Puppet is always hanging around her. She'll know where he is for sure."

He hurried into the practice tent, where Wire Walker was on her practice wire, balancing on a bike.

"Hey - where's Puppet?" he asked her.

Wire Walker stood up on her bike. She held out her arms - balanced perfectly. "Why don't you leave him alone?" she asked.

Ringmaster glared at her. "What do you mean?"

"You're not very nice to Puppet. You're always making him do horrible things. Why, only last week you made him dance up on my high wire, and when he fell, he nearly broke his neck."

"I was only trying to make a bit more money," explained Ringmaster. "Anyway, I'm not going to make him dance on your high wire this evening - I'm going to make him dance in the fire!"

"The fire?" cried Wire Walker, almost falling from her bike. "You can't do that! He'll burn up to nothing!"

"I can do it, and I will do it!" cried Ringmaster. "Now, get down and help me look for Puppet!"

Ringmaster got everyone to look for Puppet. For hours and hours they searched, but there was no Puppet to be seen. All they discovered was a number of strings, lying in the dampness of long grass by the monkey cage.

"Puppet cut his strings off!" whispered Juggler.

"He didn't want to stay here any longer," whispered Lion Tamer.

"He's gone forever!" whispered Wire Walker.

"He's a fool!" cried Ringmaster. "How will he dance properly without his strings? His dancing will be worse than ever! And he'll hate it!"

Juggler, Lion Tamer and Wire Walker stared out beyond the circus. They stared at cool bush and green fields and high mountains. And in the distance, they spotted a tiny figure, atop a rounded hill, leaping and jumping and swinging about, full of energy, full of joy.

They realised at once that Ringmaster was wrong. Puppet's dancing was better than ever. And clearly he was loving it!

Sharing

Puppet has no control over what he does at first - he must do everything Ringmaster wants him to do. How do you think he feels about this?

Ringmaster doesn't have to make Puppet do terrible things. Why does he choose to do so? What does this tell us about him?

What do you think the other members of the circus think of Puppet and Ringmaster? Why do you think so?

Puppet cuts off his own strings at the end of the story - a serious thing for a puppet to do. Why does he do this?

At the end, once his strings are gone, Puppet can be controlled no longer. He is free to choose, just like us. How do you think he feels about this? Why?

What sort of choices do you think he will make for himself? Why?

Scripture

Read the following scripture passage to the children.

Suddenly a man with leprosy came and knelt in front of Jesus. He said, "Lord, you have the power to make me well, if only you wanted to." Jesus put his hand on the man and said, "I want to! Now you are well." At once the man's leprosy disappeared. (Matthew 8:2-3)

Jesus was always making choices to heal and help those around him. What do you think he feels about those, like Ringmaster, who make choices that hurt others?

What kind of choices might God hope we make as we journey through life? Why?

Why doesn't God control us, like a puppet-master controlling his puppets, to prevent us from making choices that hurt others?

Activities

1. People Puppets

For this activity, the children will work in groups of four or six.

Half of the group will be puppets, weak and floppy, and unable to move on their own. The other half will be the puppet-masters. This group will guide the hands and arms of the bodies of the 'puppets', bringing them to life and helping them to move about.

Moving in this way, the 'puppets' should act out a short play where someone makes a choice whether to help or hurt someone else.

These plays will be shared with the group.

2. Hand Puppets

(This activity could be extended over two sessions.)

Each member of the group will make a puppet using an old sock pulled over the hand. These could be decorated with buttons, wool, cloth, felt pens, tin foil, glitter, glue, tape, etc.

In small groups, the children develop puppet shows where the puppets do mean and nasty things to each other.

After presenting their show to the group, the children should let their puppets talk to everyone, explaining why it's unfair to be forced to act in a certain way and why it's better to have the freedom to choose.

3. Multiplot Comic Strip

Remind the group that we have the freedom to make choices that can either help or hurt others. Explain that they are going to create a comic strip in which a character has to make such a choice. The comic strip will have two endings - one showing the result of a generous choice, the other showing the result of a selfish choice. The comics should be set in a place where we often find ourselves: at home, at school, in a park with friends, at a shopping mall etc.

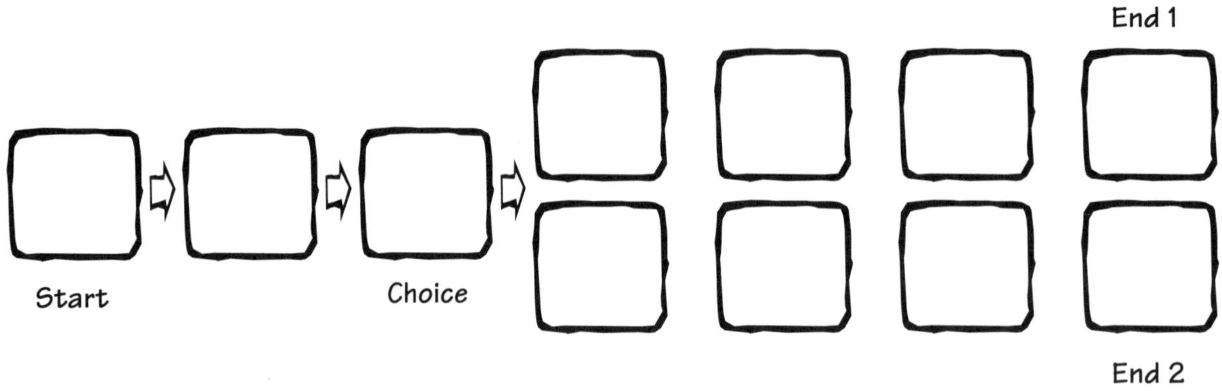

The children share the comics with the group and discuss the different endings.

4. Trapped

Give the children the following instructions.

Imagine you are a puppet, made of pegs, cloth and bits of wire. You are controlled completely by your strings, and you cannot choose what to do. The puppet-master always decides what will happen; you never have a choice of your own. Write a few sentences about your thoughts, feelings and longings. Tell what it is like to be controlled by others. Tell what you wish for most of all and why.

Draw and colour a picture of yourself, then share your work with the group.

Reflection

A puppet has no control over its movements. A puppet cannot choose its own path. A puppet cannot decide to be good, kind or generous, nor can it decide to be selfish, hurtful or cruel. A puppet has no choice at all. It is guided by the puppet-master, and has no freedom. None.

But we humans are not puppets. We are free to choose our own actions. At times we may choose to be good or kind or generous. At times we may choose to be selfish or hurtful or cruel. It is always our choice.

Sadly, we live in a world filled with suffering, and much of the pain around us is caused by selfish choices, by cruel choices. Many of us seem to hurt those around us often.

At times, we may want to call out to God the Creator, begging for the pain that fills so many lives to be taken away. But God will never remove our freedom to hurt others. God may suffer along with those we hurt, and God may hope desperately that we will choose love over hate and generosity over selfishness, but God will never, never take away our freedom to choose.

If our freedom was taken from us, God would be turning us into puppets.

Prayer

Assist the children with creating a sacred space. It may include pictures depicting peace (doves, serene landscapes, ocean scenes, animals playing etc).

For this prayer, either a pair of hand puppets or several hand puppets will be needed. Selected children say the puppet parts of the prayer, using the puppets to act out their parts. The rest of the group prays the prayer responses.

Group:
God our maker, we are not puppets.
You have given us the freedom to do as we wish.
You have given us the freedom to choose.

Puppets:
But we have no choice, like you people do.
We have no freedom.
Everything is decided for us.
We have no choice at all.

Group:
God our maker, you have given us the freedom to choose what we say.
We can say kind things.
We can say friendly things.
We can say cheerful things.
But we can say cruel, hurtful things, too.

Puppets:
We have no freedom about what we say.
Our puppet-masters decide for us.
They decide if we're loud or quiet.
They decide if we're cruel or kind.
We have no choice at all.

Group:
God our maker, you have given us the freedom to choose what we do.
We can be honest.
We can be trustworthy.

We can be helpful.
But we can be sneaky and dishonest, too.

Puppets:
We have no freedom about what we do.
Our puppet-masters decide for us.
They decide if we jump or sway.
They decide if we're sneaky or pleasant.
We have no choice at all.

Group:
God our maker, you have given us the freedom to choose how to treat others.
We can treat those around us with kindness.
We can treat them gently.
We can treat them with love.
But we can treat them cruelly and selfishly, too.

Puppets:
We have no freedom about how we treat others.
Our puppet-masters decide for us.
They decide if we play or fight.
They decide if we're cruel or kind.
We have no choice at all.

Group:
God our maker, thank you for making us different from puppets.
Thank you for giving us the ability to choose.
Please help us use our gift of freedom wisely,
so that we help rather than hurt those around us.
Help us to always choose well.
Amen.

The prayer time concludes with the group singing the song, ***We've Got the Power***.

Song

We've Got the Power

Damien Halloran & Maria Millward

You give us courage
For each choice we make,
Strength along each road we take,
Help to learn from each mistake,
But we've got the power (the power to choose),
We've got the power!

Chorus:

We've got the power,
We've got the freedom to choose.
We've got the power,
You know we cannot lose!
We've got the power,
Hey, have you heard the news?
We've got the freedom and the power to choose,
The power to choose!

You give us fam'ly,
And good friends to know,
Love and laughter as we go,
Time to wonder,
Room to grow.
But we've got the power (the power to choose),
We've got the power!

Chorus x 2

And if we want to we can make this day a better day!
(We have the freedom, we have the power today!)
And if we want to we can show this world a better way!
(What do you say?)

Chorus x 2

Action

Today I will choose to do at least one caring act for someone who is outside my immediate family or close circle of friends.

Gifts Freely Given

Unit 3

Overview

God gives us many gifts in our lives. We do not always appreciate these gifts. When we talk to God we have a tendency to ask for things. People have been doing so for the past two thousand years; it is a common trait. Even Jesus did so in times of desperation (Mark 14: 32-37).

For children, asking for things is a natural part of their developing relationship with God. This can test their faith at times, for they do not always receive what they ask for in prayer.

This unit focuses on the fact that those who love us could not possibly meet our every request without risking hurting us. It challenges the children to consider this in relation to God. They will see that we often take for granted the precious gifts we have been freely given - gifts like life itself - while demanding things that may prove detrimental to ourselves or those around us. It shows that while making requests of God is fair, expecting a quick and automatic delivery of every request is not fair at all. It encourages them to understand that God is listening even when we don't receive exactly what we ask for.

In the following story, ***Rag Doll***, a young girl asks a company representative to send her a specific gift. For some time, she fails to receive what she asks for, and some of the things she does receive result in unexpected consequences.

The reflection encourages the children to consider the precious gifts they have already received, and to think about what might go wrong if those we love did give us everything we might request.

Outcomes

The children will:

- **identify the good things in their lives that are real gifts from God - things that they often take for granted.**
- **discuss why God does not give them everything they might ask for.**
- **understand that the things they want may not necessarily be good for them.**

Getting Started

There are many things we all want in life, things such as new clothes, trips to exciting places, and wonderful new toys. Often we seem to be asking for things almost endlessly. We ask friends, parents and God for the things we want or the things we believe will make us happy.

In the following story, ***Rag Doll***, a girl asks for a special toy. For a long time, she doesn't get what she wants, and some of the things she does receive cause problems for members of her family.

Story

Rag Doll by John O'Brien

5 June

Dear Rolla-the-Clown,

Mum showed me your ad in the paper and I read it very carefully. It said that your company, Galaxy Toys, is giving away free gifts to children who write to you before the end of July. It said that we could select any gift we wanted from your toy list. I have looked very carefully at the list of gifts, and have decided I would like a rag doll. (You will note that I have circled 'Rag Doll' on the list very clearly - just as you said in your instructions.)

I think it is nice of you to give away free toys. I think it is nice of you to let us choose which toy we want.

Thank you.

Yours sincerely,

Monica Higgins

19 June

Dear Rolla-the-Clown,

Thank you for sending me a squeaking duck. I'm a bit old for squeaking ducks, so I gave it to my cousin Joel, who's just a baby. He threw it at Aunty Mary, hitting her in the eye. Then Uncle Terry trod on it and thought it was a mouse. He screamed, and I think he almost had a heart attack!

I'm writing again because in my first letter I asked for a rag doll. Perhaps you sent me a squeaking duck by mistake. If you would send me a rag doll this time, I would be most happy.

Yours sincerely,

Monica Higgins

30 June

Dear Rolla-the-Clown,

It was most kind of you to send me a Ninja sword. My brother, Danny, loved it very much. He hit me on the head with it, and then hit Mum on the leg. Then he tried to chop off Harry's tail. So Dad took it and broke it into a hundred pieces. Danny wasn't very happy. But Mum and I were. And so was Harry!

I guess you made another mistake. You see, I didn't ask for a Ninja sword. I asked for a rag doll. Would you please send me one?

Yours sincerely,

Monica Higgins

14 July

Dear Rolla-the-Clown,

Yesterday your kangaroo horn arrived. It's the first kangaroo horn I've ever seen. I gave it to my cousin Edmund, because he likes loud things. He started blowing it at once and simply wouldn't stop. After a while, Uncle Graeme went out for a walk, Aunty Ann shoved cotton wool in her ears and the man from next door came round and asked us what was the matter with the dog. We had to go home after that because Mum was getting a headache, but for all I know, Edmund might still be blowing that kangaroo horn.

Anyway, I'm writing to you for the fourth time because I actually wanted a rag doll. You said in your ad that we could choose any gift that we wanted. Remember? I think it's a bit mean of you not to send me a rag doll. Every day I go out and check the mail, hoping to find a rag doll, but all I find are kangaroo horns and things like that. I hope my rag doll arrives next week.

Yours sincerely,

Monica Higgins

27 July

Dear Rolla-the-Clown,

Well, you got it wrong again! I don't believe you! How could you send me Slime the Octopus when I asked for a rag doll?

I was so angry that I gave Slime the Octopus to my cousin Veronica. And Veronica tossed him into Aunty Ann's bath water, just before dinner-time. And two minutes later, did Aunty Ann scream! She threw Slime out through the door, where he landed on the dog. The dog yelped with fright, and tore away, right under Uncle Graeme's feet. Down went Uncle Graeme! And down went all the plates and things he had been carrying to the table. You wouldn't have believed the mess! The only good thing was that he fell right on the kangaroo horn, breaking it in two. Anyway, later on Aunty Ann told me that I was never, never to give my cousins any more gifts. Never!

I'm sick of writing to you, Rolla-the-Clown. I think you must be a horrible clown, because no matter how many times I write, you never send me what I ask for. Well, I don't want one of your stupid rag dolls any more. I really don't. I don't want anything else from you, and I will never, never laugh at a clown again. This is the last time you will hear from me, for I will certainly not be writing to you any more!

Yours sincerely,

Monica Higgins

9 August

Dear Rolla-the-Clown,

I'm very sorry about what I said in my last letter. I think you must be a nice clown after all, even though you do make lots of mistakes. And thank you a thousand times for sending me such a lovely rag doll. She's just wonderful!

Yours sincerely,

Monica Higgins

P.S. I'm going to call her Brittany.

Sharing

How do you think Monica feels when the first wrong toy arrives? Why?

How do you think she feels after the fourth wrong toy arrives? Why?

Monica doesn't give up easily - she keeps trying, over and over again. Do you think this is a good thing? Why or why not?

How do some of the toys she is sent cause problems? Which are the most unexpected or surprising problems that occur?

Scripture

Jesus suggested we should ask God for the things we need. He even did so himself - but he realised that God would not always give us everything we asked for.

Jesus walked on a little way. Then he knelt down on the ground and prayed, "Father, if it's possible, don't let this happen to me! Father, you can do anything. Don't make me suffer by getting me to drink from this cup. But do what you want and not what I want." (Mark 14: 35-36)

Just as Monica asks Rolla-the-Clown for something she wants, Jesus is asking for something from God.

What might Jesus be asking for?

His last sentence, "But do what you want and not what I want", is saying something important.

What do you think it means?

Why do you think he said it?

Activities

1. Wish List

Hand out a piece of paper to each child. Tell the children to write a heading: 'Things I Want'.

Tell them to draw pictures of three, four or five things they would really like to be given.

Once they have finished, ask the children to select one thing that could cause problems if it was received. The children take turns to explain to the group the problems that may be encountered, and why their parents or God might not see it as such a good thing for them to have.

2. Gifts Going Wrong

Divide the children into small groups. Instruct them to prepare short plays on the following theme:

Someone desperately wants something (a toy, a piece of sports gear, a trip somewhere, etc). They nag and nag their parents and finally get whatever they want, but the thing causes unexpected difficulties and problems, until the person realises they would have been better off without it.

Present the plays to the group and discuss.

3. True Gifts

Have the children consider what things they might ask God for if they could have anything they might desire. List these things on a large sheet of paper.

Ask the children to name the important gifts God has already given them. Point out that these may be gifts that are often taken for granted (e.g. life, love, friends, health, family etc). Add these things to the initial list.

Ask the children to rewrite the entire list, ordering all the things on it from the most important to the least important. Afterwards, ask them to explain to the group why they put things where they did.

Reflection

Many of us have so much, but it is never enough. Very often we want more: the latest toys or clothing, new sports equipment or computer games, extra money. We want to be different, better at things, smarter, faster, stronger, thinner, more confident, more popular. And when we do get some of the things we want, we soon dream up new wishes and longings. We have so much, but for some of us it is never enough.

We do our best to get the things we want. We nag parents, friends, relatives, and God, and we're disappointed when the things we request do not appear.

Perhaps we should slow down a little. Perhaps we should consider the good things and wonderful people already filling our lives. Perhaps we should be thankful that we are far richer than most.

And when we do ask for more, we should remember that some things may do us more harm than good. Some things may hurt or irritate or upset those around us. Some things may leave us worse off in ways we could never guess.

Those who care for us will never give us everything we want. They will happily give us much, but they won't give us everything we want.

Not if they really love us.

Prayer

Two boxes will be required for this prayer time. One should have a slot in the top, to form a 'letterbox' and the other be an attractive 'gift box' containing individual cards with written messages of love and affirmation from the Bible.

For example:

I have carved you on the palm of my hand. (Is 49: 16)
You are precious in my eyes. (Is 43: 4)
Each hair on your head is counted. (Mt 10: 30)
Do not be afraid, I am with you. (Is 43: 5)

Explain to the children that they are going to write short letters to God, letters that will be part of the shared prayer. Have them ask God, in their letters, for something they really want, something they consider important. Have them explain in the letter why they want this thing. In addition, ask them to express in the letter, as Jesus did, a realisation that God always listens to them in prayer, but that in God's wisdom their request may not be granted.

Once the letters are complete, invite the children to sit quietly around the letterbox. Explain to them that while they will be invited to share their letter as part of the prayer, they are not obliged to do so. They may choose, instead, to simply 'post' it along with the others, as a silent way of contributing.

After all the children have shared and/or 'posted' their letters to God, the final prayer is prayed. The children are then invited to choose a card from the 'gift box' to take with them to keep.

One of the children reads aloud the following prayer.

Dear God,
We write to you today, asking for things that are important to us.
All of us have hopes and dreams for the future, and our letters describe just a few small parts of our hopes and dreams.

We know that we have already received many great gifts without asking for them. While we will not receive everything we ask for, we know that you will always provide us with what we truly need.

We know that whatever the future may bring, you will always listen to us, and it is with that knowledge that we offer these letters.

Thank you, God, for listening when we talk to you.
Thank you for all the good things you provide for us.
We trust that you know best and we trust that you will continue to provide for us always.
Amen.

The prayer time concludes with everyone singing, ***Good Things***.

Unit 3

Song

Good Things

Damien Halloran & Maria Millward

Chorus:
Good things, (good things)
Are coming our way, (are coming our way).
Good things, (good things)
God sends us today! God says, "What shall I send to all of my friends?
I'll send good things, (send good things)
I'll send good things, (send good things)."

God is glad to have made us,
Oh, so glad to have made us.
Many gifts God sends us every day,
Every day, those

Chorus
God is glad to be with us,
Oh, so glad to be with us.
God is always listening when we pray,
Every day, those

Chorus
Praise our God for the good things,
Thank our God for the good things,
Celebrate the gifts God sends today,
Every day, those

Chorus

Following the prayer, the letterbox could be left in a 'sacred space' until the next session, when the letters could be handed back to the children.

Action

Each night this week, I will write down three things I can thank God for.

Bullies Big and Small

Overview

Bullying is something that most people experience at some stage through childhood, as a victim, a perpetrator or a witness. For a significant number of children, bullying is a drawn-out, traumatic experience that can inhibit their development.

Unit 4

Sadly, people have a tendency to be easily led, and children are quickly persuaded to follow the crowd. Because of this, the victims of bullying are often picked on by many. This is frequently apparent at school, or wherever children gather. Yet, many children who contribute to the teasing, exclusion and bullying of others are pleasant-natured, and have the potential to be far more inclusive and far less selfish in their relationships with their peers.

In this unit, the children are challenged to consider the problem of bullying, in the light of Jesus' teaching on our relationships with others.

The story, ***Joining the Library***, focuses on a boy who has been bullied in a number of ways. The follow-up discussion, activities and reflection encourage the children to consider bullying they have experienced, and to reflect on what they can do to ensure that they are not contributing to the bullying of others.

Outcomes

The children will:

- **understand that God calls all people to treat others with tolerance, kindness and respect.**
- **discuss the harmful effects of teasing, harassment and bullying.**
- **develop strategies to minimise negative behaviour such as bullying in their communities.**

Getting Started

Explain to the children that some children get picked on constantly. It may be because they're weak, shy or different. It may be for no particular reason. They may be excluded from games, be teased, laughed at or pushed around. Sometimes a boy or girl gets picked on by large groups of children. Their lives can be made a misery, through no fault of their own. We call such behaviours 'bullying', and most of us will encounter it sometimes as we grow up. It is never very pleasant, especially if it is ongoing. It's quite unpleasant, frightening - even terrifying at times.

If all of us were to treat each other as Jesus taught, with friendship, respect and love, bullying would never occur. Our world is not yet as caring as Jesus would want, and bullying is a widespread problem across our communities. The following story is about a boy who experiences a lot of bullying in his rather difficult life.

Story

Joining the Library by John O'Brien

"Excuse me," Liam said. "I'd like to join the library."

The librarian, seated at the main desk, stared up at him. "You would?"

"Oh." Liam looked down at his muddy trousers. "I fell over in the park," he explained. "I was running because these kids were after me." He grinned. "But they didn't get me. I got away."

"I see," said the librarian. She fished through a drawer at the base of her desk and found a pink form. "Take this home and have one of your parents sign it," she said. "When you bring it back, we'll issue you with a card."

Liam chewed his lip. "That mightn't be so easy," he said. "Dad's away at the moment, and Mum's not well. So...so couldn't I fill it out and sign it?"

The librarian shook her head. "I'm sorry, young man, but an adult has to sign the form. That's what the rules say."

"They sound like stupid rules," muttered Liam.

"If you want to join," the librarian said sharply, "you're going to have to follow them. You see, somebody has to be responsible for the books you borrow. If a book is lost, somebody has to agree to pay for it, and by signing the form, your parents are agreeing to take responsibility."

Liam was silent a moment, thinking about this. "But if I signed the form, I would be responsible," he said. "And I would pay for the books."

The librarian smiled at him. "What if you lost a fifty dollar book?" she asked. "How would you possibly pay for it? Do you have a spare fifty dollars lying around?"

Liam shook his head. "I'll be careful with the books," he said. "I won't lose or damage any of them. Then there'll be no need to pay."

"I'm sorry," said the librarian. She smiled again. "Why don't we fill out the form together. Then all your mother will have to do is sign it. You could bring it back tomorrow and we could issue you with a card right away."

"I don't know," Liam said unhappily. He sighed. "I suppose we could try."

"Good. Now what's your full name?"

"Liam O'Donnell."

The librarian quickly wrote this down. "And what's your address?"

"Seventy-two Hill Street."

"From the top of the valley? Do you have a brother called Mike?"

Liam nodded. "Well, I'm sorry...."

The librarian screwed up the pink form. "I'm afraid we won't be accepting any application from you until your parents pay for all the books your brother and sister have lost or damaged."

"That's not fair!" cried Liam.

The librarian glared at him. "And is it fair to other library members if we let a single family lose or damage book after book? Your sister lost six books late last year! And that older brother of yours! How he could possibly walk in here and try to return a book that was partly burnt, I just don't know!"

Liam breathed a deep sigh. "Oh, well. Mum would never have signed the form anyway. She's sick of getting those bills you keep sending her."

The librarian nodded. "I'm sorry, Liam, but that's the way things are."

"Don't worry," said Liam. "I'm used to it."

"Used to it? What do you mean?"

"The others are always causing trouble," explained Liam. "My brother's gang is always after me these days. It's because I won't keep lookout for them when they go shoplifting. Some of them tried to get me in the park. But I can outrun them mostly." He smiled briefly. "My sister's almost as bad. You know, my new teacher's really mean to me because Shauna used to swear at her last year."

"Is that right?" said the librarian.

Liam nodded. "I even got in trouble with the police a while ago. They hassled me for ages. Then they drove me home. And they said if they caught me lighting fires, they'd lock me up!"

The librarian raised her eyebrows. "Why do they think you light fires?"

"It's because my brother does!" cried Liam. "Everyone thinks I'm just like him!"

"Are you like him, Liam?"

Liam shook his head. "I never start fights or fires. I never wreck things or hurt people."

The librarian smiled. "So if you manage to join our library, you won't treat our books the way your brother and sister did?"

"Of course not," said Liam. "I must have read half the books in our school library, and I haven't damaged even a single page!"

"What? Not a single page?"

"That's right." Liam thought for a moment. "Look, I'll show you." He knelt down and opened his school bag. He fished through it, and lifted out an exercise book. "This is my writing book," he explained. "I like writing stories, you see, and I've taken really good care of it." He held it out. "See?"

The librarian took the book and flipped through it. "It's in excellent condition," she murmured. She was silent a while, reading some of Liam's work. "This is excellent, Liam! Do you work on it often?"

"Almost every day," said Liam. "I've got this secret place, in the back shed. I've cleared a space in all the junk, you see, and I write there all the time. I read there, too. The others don't know about it. So if Mike and his gang are after me, or if Dad comes home drunk, I'm safe there. I can read or write in peace, no matter what's happening in the house."

"I see." The librarian sat staring at Liam for quite a long time. Then she reached into her drawer and pulled out another pink form. She wrote his name at the top.

"It's no good filling it in for me," Liam told her. "I won't be able to get anyone to sign it."

The librarian smiled at him. "I'll sign it, Liam," she said. "I'll sign it."

Sharing

Like many children, Liam gets picked on by a group of older kids. One of these is actually his brother. Why is this happening?

What does Liam try to do about this bullying? What are some other things he could do about the bullying?

What do kids you know do when they find themselves bullied? What do you do if you find yourself bullied? Is it easy to overcome bullying? Why or why not? How might our group work together to overcome bullying?

As well as being bullied by other kids, Liam is also bullied by some adults. Who are the adults mentioned in the story who haven't treated Liam fairly? What have they done to treat him poorly? Why have they done so?

Scripture

Explain to the children that bullying is a very common experience and that it even happened to Jesus.

The men who were guarding Jesus made fun of him and beat him. They put a blindfold on him and said, "Tell us who struck you!" They kept on insulting Jesus in many other ways. (Luke 2: 63-65)

Like Liam, Jesus is getting bullied by a whole group of people. They are meant to be guarding him. They should not be bullying him. Why might they be doing so?

They are bullying him both through teasing and through physical assault. Do most bullies act in this way?

How do you think Jesus feels in this situation? Why?

How do you feel when you or someone you know gets bullied? How do you feel when you take part in the bullying of another child?

Jesus' teaching on bullying is very clear: he hopes that we will all treat others with care, respect and sympathy. How would our homes, schools and communities be better places if we all followed these teachings? How would the world be a better place if we did so?

Activities

1. Unfair Situations

On a large sheet of paper, write up some typical examples of harassment and bullying.

For example:

- A child in a class who is struggling to learn is teased and labelled 'stupid'.
- A shy young child is teased and pushed about by others who live in the neighbourhood.
- Members of a family from a different culture get excluded from games and other activities.
- A new kid at school is picked on and bullied by a group of friends trying to show off to each other.
- A popular gang of kids expects those who want to join to annoy or even fight other kids as a kind of initiation.

Have the children, in small groups, discuss and decide:

- why the bullying is taking place.
- how the victim of bullying would feel.
- how God might feel about the situation.
- what could be done to improve the situation.

The children present their conclusions to the larger group.

2. Place of Justice

Discuss briefly with the children possible reasons why teasing and bullying occur. Ask them to form pairs and to draw up short lists of guidelines a school or other group could use to ensure that teasing and bullying do not occur.

Have the pairs present their lists to the group, explaining why they have chosen their specific guidelines.

3. Anti-Bullying Sign

In this activity, the children will design and draw an anti-bullying sign, based on the popular international signage which is commonly seen in public places throughout the world. (Two sample signs appear below.)

No Smoking

No Dogs

Explain to the children the significance of signage and how the visual images cross over barriers such as language. Ask the children to copy the style of the international signs when designing their own sign.

The finished signs could be placed in prominent places around the school and/or local community. Perhaps the best designs could be sent to the local council authority for possible display in the neighbourhood.

4. Seeking Help

Brainstorm with the children and list people, places and services that are available in your area, where children who are victims of bullying can seek and find help. For example: parents, school councillor, chaplain, police, children's phone help line etc.

Provide the children with a comprehensive contact list of local, state and national services which have been set up to assist children who are being affected by bullying.

Reflection

Somewhere in the world, a boy is refusing to go to school. He is saying that he is feeling sick, that he is dizzy, that he wants to go back to bed. But he is not telling the truth. He is really too frightened to go to school. He knows he will be teased and ridiculed if he goes, for that's what happens at school to that boy. He gets teased and ridiculed there - every single day.

Somewhere in the world, a girl is creeping home the back way. She doesn't dare go along the main road. A gang that hangs out there will get her for sure if she does. Whenever that girl leaves home, she creeps along back streets, terrified that she's going to get knocked around some more by a group of kids that pick on her simply for kicks.

Somewhere in the world, isolated kids are walking around crowded playgrounds all alone, unable to join in any of the games taking place, unable to laugh and talk and fool around with the other kids, hating every moment of their long, lonely lunchtime.

Somewhere in the world, terrified children are wondering when the next beating will come. Day by day they are being persecuted by other kids their own age. Some of them carry the scars of previous beatings - bruises, cuts, even broken bones.

Somewhere in the world, kids are living nightmare lives, being hurt and bullied and exploited by adults who should be protecting them. Each new day for them brings with it the chance of new horror and pain.

But this is not the way things are meant to be. If we cared for each other the way Jesus cared for those around him, none of us would cruelly inflict pain on another person. Teasing and bullying and other forms of cruelty would be things of the past.

Prayer

For this prayer, each child will need a bubble wand made with pipe-cleaners.

An outdoor setting is an ideal place for this prayer time. Invite the children to be seated in a circle on a blanket or mat. A dish containing liquid soap is placed in the centre of the circle.

Each child is given a bubble wand. Explain that they are invited to pray a short prayer asking God to help them to bring peace to the world. (For example: God help me not to argue with my sister; Jesus, give me the courage to speak out when I see someone being bullied.) As each person finishes their prayer, they should move forward, dip their bubble wand into the liquid soap and blow a series of bubbles to symbolise the freedom that peace and caring for other people brings.

Unit 4

The children are invited to pray the following prayer.

Leader:
Kind and caring God,
At times so many of your people hurt those around them.
All of us are able to bully and tease.
We offer you the following prayers and trust that you will give us the strength to help rather than hurt.

The children pray their individual prayers and blow their bubbles.

Together the children pray the following prayer.

All:
God,
We have told you about the hurt we have seen around us.
We have asked you to guide us when we see such hurt, so we can help those who are bullied and teased.

Your son, Jesus, always treated others with kindness and care.
Please help us to follow his example.
Amen.

The children are invited to sing, ***We Will Bring Your Peace.***

Song

We Will Bring Your Peace

Damien Halloran & Maria Millward

Chorus:
We will bring your peace into the world.
We will bring your peace into the world.
With a loving hand, do the best we can,
We will bring your peace to the world.

Jesus, you ask us to be gentle.
Jesus, you ask us to be kind,
To take good care of each other,
Then your peace will be here for all to find.

Jesus, you ask us to be friendly.
Jesus, you ask us to be fair,
To take good care of each other,
Then your peace will be here for all to share.

Action

Next time I experience or witness bullying, I will go to an adult and seek help.

Riches in the Eyes of God

Overview

This unit focuses on poverty. In the story, ***The Fire-Dragon***, a mother and child struggle through a low point in their difficult lives. They have little in the way of material possessions, but they do have some of the qualities Jesus considers important. These qualities form a basis for the discussion and reflection that comes after reading the story.

Outcomes

Unit 5

The children will:

- consider and discuss the poverty in which so many of God's people are trapped.
- identify and discuss the special love and caring that Jesus displayed towards the poor.
- understand that God asks all people to share with those who are poor.
- recognise that material possessions are not necessarily a measure of happiness.

Getting Started

Many of us value things that Jesus tells us God does not value. We often value material things: money and all the good things money can buy. We are often selfish with such things and fail to see those around us who are in desperate need.

The people in the following story don't have many of the material things that so many of our families possess. They don't own very much at all, but in spite of their poverty, they do have something that is precious in the eyes of God. Think about what this might be while you listen to the story.

Story

The Fire-Dragon by John O'Brien

"Well, that's everything," said Mum, placing the last box of stuff from the car on the floor. "And about time!"

Thomas nodded. He sat back on the threadbare sofa, rubbing his fingers over a black stain that half-covered one of its fat arms.

"I wish we could have found a better place to live," Mum said. She sat down too. "But rents are very high at the moment. Even this wreck is costing a fortune."

"It's all right, Mum," said Thomas. "It's not a bad place."

Mum smiled. "You're a good boy," she said. "You've been a big help today."

Thomas smiled back. "There is something funny about this place," he said.

"And what's that?" asked Mum.

"There's no hot water," explained Thomas. "There's just one tap in the kitchen sink - and it's cold."

Mum nodded. "The only hot water's in the bathroom. There's a gas-burner by the bath."

"Oh," said Thomas.

"I suppose I should show you how it works," said Mum, standing up. She led Thomas into the bathroom and up to the burner, a rusty, silver cylinder with pipes leading in and a thin chimney leading up and out.

"You don't see them much any more, Thomas, but when I was a young girl, quite a few places had gas burners like this. Cheaper places, anyway. A lot of people couldn't afford proper hot-water systems in those days."

We can't afford a proper hot water system these days, Thomas thought. He stared at the gas-burner uncertainly. He had never seen anything like it before. It seemed almost a living thing to him. A dragon of old, old metal. A water-dragon.

"Don't worry about showing me, Mum," he said nervously. "You can do it for me if I need hot water."

"Oh, don't be silly, Thomas. I can't be lighting it for you all the time!"

Thomas sighed. But he watched, as Mum got ready to light the gas burner.

"First you turn on these taps," she told him. "They get the water running through the burner and up to the shower."

Thomas nodded. "What's the third tap for?" he asked.

"It's for the gas," explained Mum. "Before I turn that one on, I'll light a match."

She struck a match and turned the third tap on. Then she pushed the match into a little hole in the side of the cylinder. There was a sudden roar, and bright flames leapt from the bottom of the cylinder. For a brief moment they went everywhere. But then they disappeared again - back inside the cylinder, and soon after, warm water started flowing from the shower.

"See?" said Mum. "It's easy."

Thomas nodded, his eyes big. He decided the burner wasn't a water-dragon after all. It was worse than that, for it spat and breathed wild flames. It was a fire-dragon.

"You want a try?" Mum asked, turning it off.

Thomas shook his head.

"Well, let's start unpacking." Mum led Thomas from the bathroom, and they both got working.

Thomas swept away old piles of rubbish. He scooped up a group of fat beetles he found in a dusty corner and tossed them outside. He arranged all his things in his dark, little bedroom, only stopping to put on warmer clothing as the evening air grew cold.

Long after dark, Mum called out, "You'd better stop for some dinner now, Thomas. It's almost your bed-time."

"All right," Thomas called back. He hurried down to the kitchen.

"I'm heating some baked beans," Mum said. "Run and have a quick shower, and then we'll eat."

Thomas thought of the old bathroom with its terrible fire-dragon. "Oh, Mum, I don't need a shower!"

"Thomas!" cried Mum. "You're filthy! Have a shower at once! And make sure you wash your hair!"

"But, Mum!"

"Now!" Mum used her no-nonsense voice. So Thomas slowly crept off to the bathroom, grabbing pyjamas and a towel as he went.

He quickly undressed, then turned on the taps that let water feed through the gas burner and into the shower. He reached for the matches Mum had left by the mirror, pulled one out, and struck it. And he reached for the gas tap with nervous fingers.

But Thomas was unable to turn on the tap. He was unable to push the match through the little hole. The thought of all those leaping flames, bursting out everywhere, was too much. He stepped back, blowing out the match, and for a long time he stood shivering in the cold night air, wondering what to do.

Then he smiled. "I know," he whispered. "I'll tell Mum I've forgotten how to use it. I'll ask her to show me again."

He hugged his towel about him, and hurried down to the kitchen, his feet dancing over the cool floorboards. But he didn't find Mum in the kitchen. There was a smell of burning there, and a pot of half-blackened baked beans, but no Mum.

"Where are you, Mum?" Thomas called softly. He crept across the kitchen and peered through the lounge room door.

Mum was sitting on the sofa, her hands over her eyes. She was sobbing and sobbing, as though it was the worst day in all her life.

But they're only baked beans, Thomas thought, his heart thumping. Why is Mum so worried about baked beans?

He realised now that he couldn't ask her to light the burner. She would go wild if he did. Mum got angry very quickly when she was upset. He would just have to light it himself.

When he returned to the bathroom, Thomas stood by the burner for ages. His stomach twisted itself into tight knots. Twice he lit matches and reached out to start the burner, but both times he blew the matches out again. He didn't dare light the thing. He just didn't dare.

He stood for some time, not sure what to do. Then he reached out to touch the water raining down from the shower. It was so cold he shivered when he felt it. But he knew that anything would be better than lighting the fire-dragon. Anything.

Grabbing the soap and shampoo, Thomas climbed under the icy stream of water. It hit him like a sudden shock. It took his breath away. Never before had he imagined that water could be so painful. But he forced himself to remain there, and began soaping all the dirt off his arms and legs.

Soon Thomas was trembling wildly. He felt almost sick from the cold. He finished cleaning himself, then put his head under the freezing stream, so he could wash his hair. He gasped as it sucked warmth from his face, but poured shampoo into his blue-white hands, and began to scrub his hair.

He was so full of cold that he didn't hear his mother at the door. He didn't hear her enter and step up to the bath. He only became aware of her when the freezing stream was suddenly gone.

"Thomas!" Mum cried. She grabbed the towel and draped it around him. "Are you crazy? You're blue with cold!"

Thomas hugged the towel close. He was shivering so much he could barely speak. He felt his eyes fill with tears. "I don't like that thing, Mum," he sobbed. "I'm too scared to light it! I tried, but I can't!"

"Oh, Thomas." Mum sat on the edge of the bath, and hugged him tight. "Why didn't you ask me?"

"You'd have gone mad, Mum."

Mum scratched her fingers through his shampoo-filled hair. She sat thinking for a while. Then she helped him from the bath and reached for the matches. "I don't suppose it'll kill me to light it a few extra times a week, will it?"

Thomas shook his head. He smiled up at Mum. And soon she was gone, and he was stepping into a lovely warm shower of water. He sighed with delight, while the fire-dragon roared beside him.

Sharing

Thomas and his mother are poor and struggling. What are some things in the story that tell us this?

What does Thomas think of his new home?

Thomas doesn't own very much. What are some things that many children possess that he is probably missing out on?

Both Thomas and his mother get upset in the story. What exactly upsets Thomas? What upsets his mother? How do they try to help each other? Though they don't own very much, they do have real love for each other. How do we know this?

Jesus suggested that we shouldn't worry about collecting large amounts of money, wealth and material things. He said that qualities like love, faith and caring were far more important. What might he think of this small, struggling family? Why?

What riches might God see this little family possessing?

Scripture

Jesus also highlighted the importance of helping those who are in need:

'When you give a feast, invite the poor, the crippled, the lame, and the blind. They can't pay you back. But God will bless you and reward you when his people rise from death.' (Luke 14: 13-14)

What might God expect people to do to help those in desperate need like Thomas and his mother?

Discuss with the group why people like Thomas and his mother become trapped in poverty even when they are living in wealthy countries.

List the reasons suggested.

Have the children suggest ways we can assist those in our communities who are trapped by poverty.

Activities

1. Riches on Earth and Riches in Heaven

Divide the children into smaller groups. Give each group a large sheet of paper or cardboard. Tell the children to write the headings 'Riches on Earth' and 'Riches in Heaven', one on either side of the paper or cardboard.

Have the children draw, colour in, cut out and glue on suitable pictures that illustrate examples of 'Riches on Earth' and 'Riches in Heaven.'

Ask them to explain to the group what they have drawn and why.

2. Qualities to Live By

On small pieces of paper, list the following positive qualities: service, caring, generosity, honesty, kindness, joy, welcome, trust, etc.

Have each pair of children take one 'quality' and quickly develop a mime that illustrates it. Ask them to present the mimes to the group. The group tries to work out which 'quality' is being presented.

3. 'Thank You' Letters

Have the children write short letters of thanks to God, describing the many riches they have been given. They may mention both earthly riches and heavenly riches.

Ask for volunteers to share the letters with the group.

Reflection

Sometimes we do not notice the poor and needy among us. Listen to the following incident. Think about whether you would have noticed the boy in need, and consider whether you would have reacted as the girl did.

Many years ago, when I began teaching, someone started stealing from the children in my class. The first thing to go was a packet of potato chips. A girl came to me one lunchtime, and told me the chips had been taken from her bag. She wasn't very happy.

The next thing to go was a small bar of chocolate. Then an apple disappeared, then a sandwich, and another bag of potato chips.

I wasn't very happy about the thefts, and I kept my eye on the locker area, where the children kept their school bags. Before long, I saw the thief in action.

It was a boy named Danny. He crept into the locker area, glanced about to make sure nobody was near, and began searching through school bags. Soon he grabbed an orange and a little packet of biscuits.

Before Danny could escape, I confronted him and let him know that I was annoyed that he was stealing his classmates' possessions. Angrily, I asked Danny why he had been stealing.

Danny told me he'd been hungry. I soon found out his mother was not at home - she was in prison. There wasn't much to eat at home. Often he and his brother had no breakfast, and then came to school without any lunch. And often there was no dinner - unless Dad bought takeaways on his way home from the pub.

In the end I didn't punish Danny for stealing. Instead, I came to an agreement with him: I would buy him some lunch each day, and he would stop taking other kids' food.

The agreement worked well. Each new day, I would get Danny a sandwich or meat pie and some fruit, and the stealing stopped. Danny didn't need to take things anymore. Not now that he was being fed.

Then one day I fell sick with a bad cold. For over a week I stayed at home in bed. As I lay there, I worried about Danny. I realised he would be hungry again. I thought he might start stealing once more.

When I recovered, however, I got a pleasant surprise. Danny hadn't started stealing. He told me that a girl in my class, Jenny, had shared her lunch with him each day. Her friends had given him things to eat too.

Later, I asked Jenny why she and her friends had done so. She said they had seen me give Danny things to eat at lunchtime, and with me away, they had felt it was their turn to do something for him. Jenny said it wouldn't have been fair to let Danny go hungry.

I learned a lot that day. I learned that I had been teaching my students far more than I'd imagined. Apparently, I taught them something about Jesus' teachings on poverty - without even meaning to.

Prayer

For this prayer time a jug filled with water and enough plastic cups for each person will be needed. Explain to the children that during the prayer there will be short, quiet times for reflection. Ask them to use these quiet times to think about the things mentioned in the prayer, to silently pray to God about them. Ask them to do so without disturbing others, to close their eyes, or to focus on the water.

Have them sit comfortably in a circle. Place the jug and cups in the centre of the circle. Instruct the children that in this prayer time, the water will represent 'Riches on Earth'.

Quietly play the instrumental music track of ***I Will Bless You, Lord***.

One of the children is invited to read the following prayers.

Child:
Loving God,
Most of us have so much.
You have blessed us with great riches.
We have good food to eat in abundance.
We have clothing to suit every season.
We have people and places to help us when we're sick.
We have homes filled with good things of every kind.
We have schools and churches in which to learn and grow.
We have toys.
We have games.
We have so very much.

The leader pours water from the jug into all the cups except for 2-3 cups, which remain empty. The children quietly reflect.

Child:
Loving God,
Our world is full of poverty.
Many people are very, very poor.
They cannot afford food for their families to eat,
Or provide a home in which to live,
Or schools in which to learn,
Or places to go when they are sick.
Many children have few toys, few games.
They have so very little.

The leader quietly hands out a cup to each child. Some of the cups will be empty.

(Brief, quiet reflection.)

Child:
Loving God,
Your son, Jesus, loved the poor.
He helped in any way he could.
His example is something we can all try to follow.
All of us can help a little.
We can share when we meet those in need.
Share our time, our toys, our games.
Even our food and clothes and money.

Leader:
Let us raise a toast to the good things that we have all been given!

(Leader watches closely and if necessary encourages the children to share their water with those who do not have any.)

All drink the water.

(Brief, quiet reflection.)

Child:
Loving God,
Help us to show that we value the many good things with which we have been blessed.
Help us to see the poor around us, to feel for them, and to share with them.
Help us to make your world a better place, as your son Jesus did whenever he met anyone in need.
Amen.

The children sing, ***I Will Bless You, Lord,*** as a final prayer.

Song

I Will Bless You, Lord

Damien Halloran & Maria Millward

Chorus:
I will bless you, Lord,
With all my heart.
I will bless your holy name!
You are a loving God,
A forgiving God.
I will bless your holy name!

You give us all we need to live.
Our health and happiness you send.
You're always ready to forgive:
Your patient love will never end.

Chorus

You help us work for what is right.
You are our strength when we are weak,
And ever safe within your sight,
Your tender love is what we seek.

Chorus

Action

During the coming week, I will remember to do something special for someone in need, even if it means that I need to make a small sacrifice so that I can be generous.

Unit 5

A Sense of the Sacred

Overview

For most Christians, the church is the focus of communal worship. Although it is the most obvious of Christian sacred places, there are others. Key sites in the Holy Land, for example, are also sacred to most Christians because these places were significant in the lives of Jesus and his early followers.

All peoples have places of great spiritual significance. For many it may be a church, a temple or a synagogue. For others it may be the place of an important birth or death. It may be the site of a battle that brought victory or defeat to a nation. It may be a place visited by ancestors in the distant past, or a place spoken of in myths or creation stories. Indigenous peoples such as the Australian Aborigines, Native Americans and the Maoris of New Zealand have sites across their traditional lands that have been sacred to them for many thousands of years.

Sadly, some of us have been slower to respect the sacred places of others than we have to respect our own sacred places. This unit encourages the children to consider this - to affirm the value they give their own sacred places, while encouraging them to respect the sacred places of others.

In the story, ***Piper in the Sand***, a young girl discovers a place with a sense of the sacred. She puzzles over her discovery, but in the end, she realises it would be wrong to tamper with the place in any way.

Outcomes

The children will:

- **identify and discuss places that are sacred to their faith community.**
- **recognise and name places that are sacred to other cultures and other religions.**
- **understand that they should respect that which is sacred to others.**

Getting Started

If someone wanted to build a parking lot or a shopping mall on an old graveyard, there would be a public outcry. People would be horrified. They wouldn't want the bodies of their loved ones to be disturbed, and they would have every right to be upset.

We expect that people will respect the places that are sacred to us - our churches, for example, or the places where our dead are buried. In turn, we have an obligation to respect the sacred places of others, even if we, ourselves, don't value those places as they do.

In the following story, ***Piper in the Sand***, a girl who is holidaying with her family discovers a place that is very special to someone who may have lived long, long ago.

Story

Piper in the Sand by John O'Brien

"What are you doing, Sally?" Dad asked, as he lay down in the shade of the beach umbrella.

"I'm listening to something, Dad," said Sally. She knelt down, her head over the top of the deep hole she had dug in the sand. She concentrated, listening carefully, trying to catch the soft sounds she had heard moments before.

Then Sally smiled. Faintly, ever so faintly, she heard the tune again. Though slightly sad, it was as warm and gentle as a sun-drenched ocean. It seemed to Sally that someone deep underground was playing a magical flute. She reached down and scooped more and more sand out of the hole.

"Trying to get to the other side of the world?" Mum asked. She wriggled about on her beach towel until she could watch Sally.

"Not that far, Mum," said Sally. She dug a little more. Then she crouched lower, listening again.

The music was louder this time, but for some reason it seemed sadder. As the clear notes danced through her ears, Sally felt a heaviness in her heart. She sat up, wondering about it.

"Are you all right, Sally?" Dad asked her.

Sally nodded. Then she said, "Could you come over here and listen to this hole I've dug?"

"Whatever for?" asked Dad, surprised.

"Well..." Sally considered this. "I can sort of hear something in it. I want to find out if you can hear it, too."

Dad jumped up and stepped over to the hole. He crouched beside it and listened carefully. "I can hear a rushing sound," he said, after a while. "Sort of an echo of the waves, I think. But that's all."

"Oh," said Sally.

Dad stood up. "Should I have heard something else?"

"I don't know," said Sally. She knelt beside the hole, wondering why Dad hadn't heard the music. Then she reached down and began to dig some more. She dug for ages this time, and the hole got deeper and deeper and deeper.

When Sally listened again, the music was far louder than before, but how sad it had become! The melody was one of fear and worry. It told of cold fogs and icy water and too little wind. And when Sally sat up once more, she realised there were tears in her eyes.

"Sally!" cried Mum. "What's the matter?"

"Oh, Mum," said Sally. "You've got to come and listen to the hole! You've got to!"

She wiped her eyes, watching as Mum stepped to the hole, crouched down and listened. She watched as she stood up again.

"What am I supposed to hear, Sal?" Mum asked her. "The waves? The breeze?"

Sally sighed. "It doesn't matter," she said. She began to dig rapidly. She dug and dug until the hole was so deep she could only just touch the bottom. And then, all of a sudden, her outstretched hands brushed over something hard, hidden in the damp sand. She grabbed it and lifted it out.

"I wonder what this is," she murmured, brushing sand away from the object.

"They look like pipes," said Dad.

"Pipes?" said Sally.

Dad nodded. "You blow on them, to make music."

Sally looked at the pipes, which were made of reeds or something. There was a whole row of them, all joined together, quite short at one end, but gradually getting longer towards the other.

"They sound like a flute," Mum explained. "But nicer somehow."

"They look pretty old," said Dad. "Perhaps they belonged to some shipwrecked sailor."

"You could take them home," added Mum.

Sally considered this. She put her head to the hole, listening. But this time she heard nothing. Nothing at all. And suddenly she realised why the music had been getting sadder and sadder.

"I can't take them home!" she cried. "That would be stealing!"

"But, Sally," Dad protested. "These pipes may have washed up here over a hundred years ago. How can you steal from someone who's no longer living?"

"I've got to put them back!"

Her parents stared at her for a moment. Then Mum said: "Put them back if you want, dear. It doesn't really matter."

So Sally dropped the pipes back into the hole, and poured several handfuls of sand over them. Then she crouched to listen once more.

The music had returned. It was louder than ever, filling her ears with notes as clear as sparkling water and as fresh as a salty breeze. It danced through every part of her until she was trembling with delight.

There wasn't a hint of sadness about it. Not a hint.

Sharing

When did Sally first sense that there was something special about the patch of beach where her family was resting?

Did her parents sense it, too? How do you know?

When did Sally finally realise that it would be wrong to disturb this special place? What gave her this insight?

Towards the end of the story, Dad asks Sally, "How can you steal from someone who is no longer living?" Do you think it is possible to steal from the dead? How? Can you think of an example of stealing from the dead?

Do you think what Sally did at the end of the story was right?
Why or why not?

Scripture

Jesus once got very upset when he discovered that a sacred place was being used in an unfair, disrespectful manner. He was in the Great Temple in Jerusalem at the time, and he became quite angry.

Jesus went into the Temple and chased out everyone who was selling or buying. He turned over the tables of the money-changers and the benches of the ones who were selling doves. He told them, "The Scriptures say, 'My house should be called a place of prayer.' But you've turned it into a place where robbers hide." (Matthew 21: 12-13)

Jesus was angry that many people were not showing respect for the Temple. What were they doing that upset him?

How would he want us to treat our own sacred places, such as our churches? Why?

How would he want us to treat the sacred places of others? Why?

Activities

1. Our Own Precious Places

Talk with the group about places that are special for some reason (e.g. places where favourite activities take place, places where friends gather, places that are quiet retreats or refuges, peaceful gardens, favourite holiday destinations, etc).

List and/or illustrate these on a large poster.

Discuss with the children how they would feel if these places were damaged or destroyed in some way. Talk about the responsibility we have to treat the special places of others with care and respect.

2. Damaging the Sacred

Have the children, in small groups, develop short plays showing someone damaging a sacred place in some way. For example:

- demolishing a church so a shopping mall can be extended
- teenagers damaging a cemetery
- settlers building on a sacred site of indigenous peoples
- a community forcing the closure of a place of worship of a minority group

The plays should finish with someone trying to prevent the damage from occurring.

Present to the group and discuss.

3. A Variety of Special Places

Provide each child with a handful of modelling clay. Ask them to create a shape which symbolises a special place for one of the following groups.

- family
- faith community
- local community
- nation

Discuss the completed symbols with the group.

Reflection

About sixty-five years ago, authorities in Munich decided to tear down a synagogue, one of the largest in all of Germany. Enormous demolition machines, giant engines of destruction, were brought into position, and bit-by-bit the great building was reduced to a mound of rubble.

It didn't matter that the synagogue was a central place of worship for many hundreds of Jews. The Nazis, in power in Germany at the time, decided they wanted to build a parking lot on the site. They demolished the wonderful building completely.

The Nazis destroyed hundreds of synagogues during their time of rule in Germany. They vandalised Jewish cemeteries, too, along with any other place precious to Jewish people. Before ten years had passed, they had begun killing off the Jews. More than five million Jews died in the Nazi nightmare of murder and destruction unleashed on them, a nightmare that began with the desecration of sacred places.

We all hope and expect that those around us will respect the places we consider precious, the places important to us, sacred to us, and we have every right to do so. In return, other peoples have a right to hope and expect that we will respect places they consider precious, important, and sacred. The world will never be a kind, just or safe place until such respect is widely shown.

We may not understand what makes a place sacred to another culture or religion, but we still must respect that place. How can our own special places, reminding us of our own history and our own relationship with God, have any meaning to us if we deny others the right to special places of their own?

Prayer

Explain to the children that for this prayer everyone will work together to create a sacred place that will help them focus on talking to and listening to God. The children might like to bring items from home. These might include flags of other countries, religious artifacts, or other symbols of religious and/or cultural significance. Provide the children with a couple of large candles, some coloured cloth and a Bible. Allow sufficient time for the children to organise the sacred space to their satisfaction. Ask for volunteers to help with the prayer. Ask the children to be seated in a circle and light the candles.

Leader:

Loving God, we have created this special place for you and we thank you for being with us as we express our thoughts and feelings today.
We have been talking about and thinking about places that are special to us and about places that are special to others.
We know you ask us to show respect to all sacred places - our own and those of others.

Remind the children that the Bible, the Word of God, is a special part of their sacred place. Tell them that they are going to listen to two short readings. The first reading is from the Book of Psalms. The Lord is being asked to come to the Temple, the most sacred place to the ancient Jewish people.

Ask one of the children to read the Psalm.

Child:
Come to the Temple, Lord, with the Covenant Box, the symbol of your power, and stay here forever.
May your priests always do what is right;
May your people shout for joy. (Psalm 132: 8-9)

(Pause)

Tell the children that even as a boy, Jesus knew just how special the Temple was. Explain that on one occasion Jesus was simply unable to drag himself away from the Temple.

Ask one of the children to read the following passage from the Bible.

Child:
Every year, Jesus' parents went to Jerusalem for Passover. And when Jesus was twelve years old, they all went there as usual for the celebration. After Passover his parents left, but they didn't know that Jesus had stayed on in the city. They thought he was travelling with some other people, and they went a whole day before they started looking for him. When they couldn't find him with their relatives and friends, they went back to Jerusalem and started looking for him there. Three days later they found Jesus sitting in the Temple, listening to the teachers and asking them questions. (Luke 2: 41-46)

(Pause)

Leader:
God,
We know you are here with us, in this special place we have created for you, just as you were in the Temple, all those years ago.

We ask you to touch our hearts today. Help us to keep sacred all the places of worship that we might visit, and help us to see the special places of all peoples as precious.

The prayer concludes with everyone singing the song, ***Welcome to God's House***.

Song

Welcome to God's House

Damien Halloran & Maria Millward

Come into God's house today.
God is here in this house today.
We will dance, we will sing,
We will welcome you in!
Welcome to God's house today!

This house is a house of peace.
Rest awhile in this house of peace.
We will dance, we will sing,
We will welcome you in!
Welcome to God's house of peace!

This house is a house of love.
Be a friend in this house of love.
We will dance, we will sing,
We will welcome you in!
Welcome to God's house of love!

This house is a house of prayer.
Speak to God in this house of prayer.
We will dance, we will sing,
We will welcome you in!
Welcome to God's house of prayer!

This house is a house of joy.
Celebrate in this house of joy.
We will dance, we will sing,
We will welcome you in!
Welcome to God's house of joy!

Come into God's house today.
God is here in this house today.
We will dance, we will sing,
We will welcome you in!
Welcome to God's house today!

Blow out the candles and ask the children to quietly and carefully pack and fold up the things that were used to create the sacred prayer space. Alternatively, the sacred space may remain for a time as a semi-permanent focal point.

Action

In the coming week, I will ask at least one person to tell me about a place that is sacred to them and why it is special.

Accepting Differences

Overview

We humans tend to be kind, generous and loving to those close to us. With others, who are distant from us and different from us, we tend to be less charitable. Many of the world's problems, such as war, prejudice, racism, inequality, poverty and cruelty, stem from this tendency.

Children, too, can treat those who are different very poorly. A child who is different, who doesn't fit in, can be very isolated in a school playground. He or she can be teased, bullied and endlessly picked on.

This unit focuses on our relationships with those who are different. It encourages the children to consider everyone as a potential neighbour - as deserving of help and of care as our closest friends and family. In the story, ***Creature From the Stars***, a little furry creature on a distant planet tells about a spacecraft that unexpectedly crashed down from above. He tells how he helped the wounded alien inside, despite it being very different, and how the alien soon returned the favour. The unit invites the children to consider what it's like to be different and treated poorly and to think about how we might treat other people better in the future.

Unit 7

Outcomes

The children will:

- **learn that all people are created and loved by God.**
- **explore the idea that all people, no matter how different they might be, have a right to be treated with respect and justice.**
- **evaluate how they treat those whom they perceive to be different from themselves in some way.**
- **explore and discuss Jesus' teaching on neighbours.**

Getting Started

Explain to the children that we don't always treat those who are different from us very well. We sometimes stare at them, laugh at them, tease them, and exclude them from our games. We often treat them far worse than we treat our friends. This is not God's wish, for Jesus taught that we should treat anyone we come into contact with as a neighbour. He taught that we should treat our neighbours as we like to be treated ourselves.

The following story is about a family living on a distant planet. One of them meets a wounded alien. He decides to help the alien, despite it being a strange giant of a creature, and it is very lucky that he does so.

Story

Creature from the Stars by John O'Brien

"Tell us about the creature from the stars!" we cried, one cold winter's night. We tugged at Uncle Meeln's grey fur. "Tell us! Please, Uncle!"

"Very well, little ones," said Uncle Meeln. He rubbed his face with all four hands and sat down by the fire. "But after I've told you, straight to bed!"

"Of course, Uncle!" we cried, and we crept close and sat down, curling our long, furry tails about ourselves.

"Well," said Uncle Meeln. "It happened many years ago, when the great dam was leaking badly, near ready to burst and drown our lovely city."

We all shivered. Imagine the great dam bursting! It was too terrible to think about.

"Many of us were on our way up to the dam, to try to repair it," said Uncle Meeln, "when suddenly we heard a terrible noise, and an enormous, round, silver thing fell out of the sky, bursting apart as it hit the ground."

"And the creature!" cried Zlem, my sister. She scratched her shoulders with dark claws. "The creature from the stars was inside!"

"That's right," said Uncle Meeln. "And what a giant of a creature it was! More than five times my height! Yet with only two arms and two legs."

"Did it have a long tail?" I asked. It had been a long time since I had heard about the creature, and I couldn't quite remember.

"No," Uncle Meeln went on. "It had no tail. And it had very little fur - only a little on the top half of its head. And it was dressed in most unusual gold and silver clothing."

"How strange!" we all cried.

"The others went on to try to repair the great dam," said Uncle Meeln. "But I stayed behind to try to help the creature, for it was badly hurt. Strange red blood was oozing out of it in several places, so I looked after it for many days. I put healing leaves and flowers on its many wounds. I brought it water in a huge bucket, which it drained as though it was a tiny cup. And I fed it fruit from nearby trees. It took me hours to collect enough for just one meal."

"Did the creature get better?" asked Neth, my step-brother.

"It got a little better," our uncle said. "After a week or so, it could get to its feet and limp around. So I started for the great dam, where I was badly needed. I felt the creature could look after itself for a while. Strangely, the creature followed me, right up into the hills, even though it was still in pain. And we were lucky that it did, for the great dam was about to collapse. A large channel had been eaten through it by rushing water. The others had been trying to fill this channel with rocks and sand but the power of the water was so great that everything they threw in was quickly washed away. Soon, we knew, the whole dam would be eaten away, and the water would pour down into the valley, drowning our city."

"But the creature from the stars helped you!" Neth cried, and we all shivered with excitement. Uncle Meeln was coming to our favourite part of the story.

"That's right," he said. "The creature saw what we were trying to do and started to help us at once. It lifted boulders so huge that none of us would have dreamed of lifting them, not even with a dozen others helping. It staggered up to the great dam with these giant boulders and threw them in, one after another. Some of its wounds started bleeding again and it cried out in unknown words, as though it was hurting inside from the effort of moving such weights. But it did not stop. It threw boulder after boulder into the channel, filling it completely. We packed the small spaces between the boulders with rocks and dirt, and soon the leak in the dam was plugged. The city was safe. The creature from the stars had saved us."

"It is sad," said Zlem, "that you were not able to bring the creature back to the city so everyone could have thanked it."

"It is sad," said Uncle Meeln. "We planned to bring it back, but as we returned, an even bigger silver thing came down from the sky. It didn't crash like the first, but settled on the ground quite gently. Part of it opened up, and two more creatures appeared. They looked like the first one, though they were much bigger. The creature seemed pleased to see them, and ran towards them at once. Then it turned and waved to us. It hurried inside the silver thing with the others, and the thing flew swiftly skywards. No one has seen it since."

I sighed. "I can hardly believe, Uncle, that the other two creatures were even larger than the first one, for the first one was five times as tall as you. And how can any living thing be larger than that?"

Uncle Meeln raised his nearest hand and scratched my head. He smiled. "The first creature seemed big to us, little one, but my guess is that it was small to its own kind. My guess is that the two creatures that came for it were its parents. My guess is that the great dam and our wonderful city and all those living in it were saved by a young child. By a child no older than yourselves."

We all squealed with delight when we heard this. We wanted to hear the whole story again, but Uncle Meeln would have none of it. He hurried us off to bed, where we cuddled down under moss blankets, dreaming of strange and wonderful giants that in some unexplained way are able to move among the distant stars.

Sharing

What do you think might have happened to the creature if Uncle Meeln hadn't helped it? Why?

Why might Uncle Meeln have decided to help it?

The kids seem to like hearing their uncle talk about the creature. How do you think they would react if they came across another of the creatures? Why?

The word 'alien' is often used to represent a creature from another world, but it actually means different, foreign or from another place. Uncle Meeln treated the hurt creature very well, but very often we don't treat those we meet who are different all that well. What are some unfair ways we treat outsiders at times? Why might we do this?

Have you ever been an outsider who has been treated poorly by others? When? Where? How did you feel?

Scripture

Jesus wants us to treat everyone we come into contact with well. Jesus said that a most important commandment is:

Love your neighbour as you love yourself. (Matthew 22:39)

He also said, through the parable of the Good Samaritan, that our neighbours are those who most need our help, even if they are quite different from us. In this story a man is travelling along a road, when robbers attack and beat him. Important, well respected people do not offer help when they see him, but a Samaritan, who is considered an outsider, generously helps the man.

After Jesus told this story, he asked, "Which one of these three people was a real neighbour to the man who was beaten up by robbers?"
The teacher answered, "The one who showed pity."
Jesus said, "Go and do the same!" (Luke 10: 36-37)

According to Jesus' teaching, how should we treat those who are different? Can you think of some situations when we need to try harder to put his teaching into practice?

Activities

1. Individual Differences Game

A bag of potatoes, enough for each child, will be required for this activity.

The following game is a good way for the children to appreciate individual differences.

Each child selects a potato and looks at it carefully, noting its special characteristics. Everyone places their potatoes in a pile and mixes them up. Each child then tries to find 'his/her' potato.

Explain that although all potatoes may look alike, each one possesses differences that make all of them unique. Discuss with the children how this is also true with people.

2. Alien

The word 'alien' means 'different' or 'outsider'. Discuss with the group times when some of them have felt different, like an outsider.

Have members of the group role-play situations where someone is being excluded, teased or bullied because they are an outsider who is different in some way.

For example:

- a new kid at school
- someone who doesn't speak English well
- someone with a disability

After each role-play, discuss the following with the group.
Who was being treated poorly? Why?
How do you think they felt? Why?
How might all the others in the play have felt? Why?
Have you ever experienced a situation like this? When?
If we followed Jesus' hopes for us, how would this situation have been different?

3. Moving to a Distant Planet

Imagine your family has moved to an alien planet and you have to start going to an alien school. Write an account of your first day at school. Include an incident where a group of aliens are mean to you and tell how you feel about it. Include, also, an incident where aliens are nice to you and how you feel about it.

Afterwards, read the accounts to the group and discuss.

Reflection

We all feel different sometimes. We all feel alone, vulnerable, frightened. It might be because we move to a new neighbourhood, or start at a new school. It might be because we look different in some way, or sound different, or because we belong to a different group, culture or religion from most of the people around us.

We desperately want to be accepted. We want others to like us, to talk to us, to let us take part in their games, but this doesn't always happen. Sometimes people begin to make fun of us and tease us. Then others join in. It can get so bad, we can almost wish the ground would open up and swallow us. We desperately want it all to stop. If we are outsiders, it will sometimes seem that we're being picked on by almost everyone.

This is not God's wish for us, or for anyone else. Though we cannot stop others from treating us cruelly, we certainly can make sure that we don't treat others cruelly. We can try to accept those who are different. We can talk to them and let them join in our games. We can make them feel comfortable and accepted. We can treat them as Jesus told us we should: the very way we would like everyone else to treat us. By doing so, we'll be making a little corner of God's vast universe a fairer and happier place for all.

Prayer

A wide range of shoes, of various sizes, colours and styles, will be needed for this prayer time (e.g. old boots, stilettos, wooden clogs, knitted booties, wet weather boots, school shoes, sandals, jogging shoes, slippers etc).

Have the children sit in a circle. The shoes are placed inside the circle with a Bible and a large focus candle.

Remind the children that they have been talking about appreciating differences among people, and how they might better communicate and relate with those who are different.

Tell the children that they are going to participate in a creative prayer time. Explain that they will be invited to reflect on what it might be like to walk around in another person's shoes. Tell them that they will need to imagine how that person might think, feel and act in their particular situation.

Settle the children and light the focus candle.

Leader:

We have before us the Bible, a candle and some shoes. God's word reminds us that we are all children of God. The candle symbolizes Jesus, whose light helps us to see through the eyes of others, and the different kinds of shoes remind us that many different people make up God's family.

Ask the children to focus on one shoe that they see before them, imagining that they are the owner of that shoe. Tell them to reflect quietly on their answers to the following questions:

Who are you?
How old are you?
Where do you live?
What is your family like?
What things do you like to do?
What things make you afraid?
What are your hopes and dreams?

All:

God our Maker,
You have created us and all people in your image and likeness. Help us to look beyond outward appearances and not to fall into the trap of judging others who are different from us. Help us to remember that differences are not a bad thing. Let us see that each person is gifted, unique and loved by you. Help us to remember that your son, Jesus, commands us to love one another as we ourselves want to be loved.
Amen.

Invite the children to sing, ***Do to Others***.

Song

Do to Others

Damien Halloran & Maria Millward

Do to others as you would have them do to you.
Say to others as you would have them say to you.
Think before you speak and act,
We're all God's children, that's a fact, so
Do to others as you would have them do to you.

Do to others as you would have them do to you.
Say to others as you would have them say to you.
Walk a while in others' shoes,
It's easy then to always choose to
Do to others as you would have them do to you.

Bridge:

Different eyes we have to see,
And different points of view,
With different hopes and different dreams
For you and me, for me and you,
And...

Different gifts we have to share
To help each other see
That all of us must learn to care
For each one in God's family,
And...

Do to others as you would have them do to you.
Say to others as you would have them say to you.
Think before you speak and act,
We're all God's children, that's a fact, so
Do to others as you would have them do to you.
Walk a while in others shoes,
It's easy then to always choose to
Do to others as you would have them do to you.

Action

Next time I am tempted to make fun of someone who is different from me, I will try to put myself in his/her shoes and offer a compliment instead.

When Things Go Wrong

Overview

Things often go wrong. The world is not a just place, a fair place, or a predictable place. No amount of planning and preparation will ensure that things run smoothly. Problems and setbacks will affect us all, right through our lives, though we do have some control over how we react to them.

For children, even minor setbacks can be difficult, and serious problems can prove heartbreaking. Children, quite naturally, often have a self-centred view of the world. They can be very aware of things that are not going right for them, and hurt easily, but their awareness does not always extend to the needs of those around them.

This unit opens this issue for exploration. It tries to show children that problems affect us all from time to time, and that gospel values can guide us through the difficulties we encounter. These values can help us to view the difficulties of others with a sympathetic and charitable eye.

Outcomes

Unit 8

The children will:

- **appreciate that all people will encounter problems, difficulties and challenges as they journey through life.**
- **understand how Jesus reacted to problems and difficulties - both his own problems and those of others.**
- **realise that they have a Christian duty to assist those around them who are encountering any form of serious difficulty.**

Getting Started

All people occasionally experience difficulties in life. We have problems at home, at school or with our friends. Difficulties like this are a normal part of life, but we still find them hard to cope with. At times, it seems that things go wrong for us all too often.

In the following story, ***Apples***, a boy living on a distant planet thinks of a wonderful way to help his mother. Unfortunately, when he puts his plan into action, he encounters an unexpected difficulty, and for a while, it seems to him that everything is ruined.

Story

Apples by John O'Brien

"I wish I had an apple," Mum said one afternoon. "A crisp, red apple, cool and crunchy. I'd do anything for an apple."

"Apples must be nice, Mum," said David. "You're always going on about them."

"They're nicer than anything you could imagine, David," Mum sighed. "I don't mind living here on Arruth. I don't mind living a thousand light years from Earth. But I do wish I could have an apple every now and then."

"Are apples as good as preens, Mum?" asked David.

Mum smiled. "They're even better."

David considered this. He couldn't imagine anything tasting as good as preens. If apples tasted even half as good, they must be fantastic.

Suddenly he had an idea. It was Mum's birthday in a few days. Maybe he should try to get her an apple for it. She would be ever so happy if he managed to do so. And with luck, he just might be able to find one at the spaceport.

"I'm going out!" David cried. He ran to his room and emptied his moneybox. "I'm going to watch some spaceships take off!"

"Don't be late for dinner!" Mum called after him.

"I won't!" David ran out the door. He ran down the road, just managing to catch the next airbus.

When he got to the spaceport, he didn't go to the observation level, where he often watched giant ships launch themselves into space. Instead, he crept into the dark lower levels, where cargo from many parts of the galaxy was unloaded.

"Where might I find an apple?" he asked himself, and he crept through dimly lit tunnels, looking about in all directions.

Then David smiled. Ahead was a man with black skin and an even blacker beard - a man from Earth. He was talking to a creature with pinkish scales and thin white teeth.

"Please, sir," whispered David, creeping close to the pair. "I want to buy an apple. Do you know where I can get one?"

Slowly the man shook his head. "I'm afraid I can't help you. I'm working on a Linth ship, and we carry little in the way of Earth supplies. I'm sorry."

Suddenly the man's friend nudged David with a dark claw. "I can assist, young one," it said in a hissing, whispery voice. "Go to the lowest level. There you will find a group of Vreng. The Vreng often trade with Earth ships, for they like Earth weapons and Earth food. Perhaps they can help you."

"Thanks," said David, starting away from the pair. He hurried to the nearest elevator. He took it right down to the deepest level, where it was so dark he could barely see. And he nervously crept along deserted tunnels, wondering what the Vreng might look like.

After a while, he stopped. Ahead was a group of thin, grey beings. Their eyes were blood-red, and their rumbling voices echoed through the darkness.

They stopped talking and glared at him. "What do you want?" one of them snapped.

"I.... I want to buy an apple, sir," said David, his heart thumping. "An apple from Earth. Would you have one?"

The Vreng grunted. It hurried out a side door. A moment later, it returned with something green between its thin fingers. "Here you are," it said. "One apple. Slightly chilled and in perfect condition. It will cost you half a gold piece."

"What?" cried David. He knew that all his money, which he had saved and saved for months, was worth barely a quarter of a gold piece. There was no way he could buy the apple.

"Where's the payment?" snapped the Vreng.

"I don't have enough money," whispered David. "Would you have any cheaper apples?"

"Our apples have been shipped across a thousand light years! Do you expect us to give them away?"

David shook his head. He sighed, and turned to retreat up the tunnel.

"Wait!" cried the Vreng. "I don't know why, but I feel generous today.

Perhaps I will sell you an apple for half price. One that's in....in not as good condition as this."

"You will?" said David, turning around. He watched the Vreng hurry through the door. Soon it was back again, a black plastic bag in its hand.

"Give me the payment!"

David nervously handed over the money, took the bag, and turned to hurry away. Behind him, the Vreng gave off howls of laughter.

David started running and didn't stop until he was in the safe, upper sections of the spaceport.

When outside once more, waiting for another airbus, David opened the plastic bag. Then he frowned. The apple wasn't red or green, as he had been expecting. It was brown. Perhaps it was a type his mother had never mentioned before. He pushed his hand into the bag and picked it up.

The apple fell apart in his hand. Most of it slipped through his fingers, a brown, soggy mess. The apple was rotten. The creatures had sold him an apple that was useless.

David moaned softly. He knew he couldn't possibly give the filthy apple to his mother. It would make her more miserable than before. And he knew he would never dare go back and complain to the Vreng.

He wiped away the tears that were beginning to trickle down his cheeks. Then he threw the plastic bag at a nearby rubbish bin. It all seemed terribly unfair. He had simply been wanting to make his mother feel better, and the creatures had cheated him out of all his money.

David wiped his eyes again. He sensed something on the end of his finger. He gazed down at it. Whatever could it be?

Then David smiled. Apples had seeds inside them - his mother had said so several times. The object on his finger was an apple seed.

David reached for the plastic bag. He carefully placed the seed back inside it, his smile growing wider and wider. Suddenly he knew that he would be able to give his mother a gift far more precious than just an apple.

Sharing

Why was an apple such a great present for David to get for his mother?

Why wasn't it such an easy present to actually find?

David takes a risk when he goes into the deepest parts of the spaceport.

What is this risk?

Why does he go there anyway?

Why do you think the Vreng cheat him?

How might David feel once he's outside and he discovers he has bought an apple that is rotten?

Can you think of a time when you, like David, felt upset because things unexpectedly went wrong? What happened? How did you feel about it? What did you do?

Things go wrong for everyone at times. Even Jesus encountered serious problems, some of them quite unexpected.

Scripture

Jesus left and returned to his home town with his disciples. The next Sabbath he taught in the Jewish meeting place. Many of the people who heard him were amazed and asked, "How can he do all this? Where did he get such wisdom and power to work these miracles? Isn't he the carpenter, the son of Mary? Aren't James, Joseph, Judas and Simon his brothers? Don't his sisters live here in our town?" The people were very unhappy because of what he was doing. And so they rejected him.
(Mark 6: 1-3)

Jesus couldn't work any miracles there, except to heal a few sick people by placing his hands on them. He was surprised that people didn't have faith.

Why are the people rejecting Jesus? How might he feel about this? Do you think he was expecting to be rejected? Why or why not?

Then Jesus went to the villages around there, teaching the people.
(Mark 6: 5-6)

Things did not go so well for Jesus in his home village, but he did not let this affect his mission. At once he continued preaching in neighbouring villages.

What might this tell us about how to react to our own difficulties?

Activities

1. Everyday Problems

Develop with the group a list of everyday places where things could go wrong. Alternatively, provide the group with a list.

For example:

- shopping at the mall
- during a test in the classroom
- while travelling with the family
- in the playground at school
- on a walk with friends
- watching TV with brothers and sisters

Divide the children into small groups. Ask each group to develop a play based on an idea from the list. In the play, something should go wrong for at least one of the participants.

Present the role-plays to the group. As each problem is encountered, halt the plays and discuss the situation with the group:

What's going wrong?
How do you think the characters might feel?
What might happen next?
How could some of the characters improve the situation or help solve the problem?

Following each discussion instruct the children to finish the play.

2. Others in Need

Explain to the children that we all have problems and difficulties, and that very often others help us through them. Give an example or two. A personal example might be effective. Alternatively, talk in general terms, such as teachers helping kids at school.

Ask the children to make a list of all the people they can remember who have helped them in some way. Once they've finished, ask them to select one name from the list, and write a paragraph explaining what the problem was, how the person helped them, and how they felt about it.

Afterwards, invite the children to share their writing with the group.

3. The 'Human Knot' Game

Explain to the children that as followers of Jesus, we are called to help those around us when things appear to be going wrong for them.

Instruct the children to gather closely in a group. Each person takes a hand of two different people who are not standing next to him or her. Tell the children to undo the human knot without releasing handholds. To do so, they will need to twist and turn in order to help each person to stay connected.

After the game, encourage the children to share their experiences with the group.

Did anyone experience difficulty holding on? What happened?

How did it feel to be pulled in many directions?

How did you respond when others were having difficulty?

4. A Caring God

Explain to the group that throughout his life Jesus was sensitive to those around him, spending much of his time on earth helping people cope with serious difficulties. Together with the group, develop a list of examples of Jesus helping others. These might include:

- healing a Roman Officer's servant
- calming a storm
- feeding the hungry
- giving sight to the blind

Ask the children to select one incident from the list and to draw and colour a picture of it.

Invite the children to speak about their pictures.

Reflection

Introduce the fable, ***Two Men and a Bear***, by reading the following introduction.

How good a friend are you? Do you help your friends in times of need? Any true friend will help those with problems. In the following fable, by Aesop, a man discovers the true nature of a friend.

Two Men and a Bear by Aesop

Two men were out for a walk in the country one day. Suddenly, one of them saw a bear nearby. Without saying a word of warning to his friend, he turned and ran to a nearby tree. He quickly climbed it to safety.

By the time the second man saw the bear, it was too late. The bear was rushing straight towards him.

With a cry of fear, the man collapsed to the ground, pretending to be dead. He hugged his frightened arms around his body and held his breath.

The bear stepped close to the man, sniffing at his eyes and ears and body. But it didn't want to eat a dead person, so it went away, hunting for a more tasty meal.

Once it had gone, the first man climbed down from the tree. He hurried close to his friend. "I can't believe it!" he cried. "It almost seemed that the bear was whispering in your ear!"

"It was! It was!" cried the second man.

"Is that so?" said the first man, amazed. "And what did it tell you?"

"It told me," the second man replied, "not to travel with friends who are as thoughtless and cowardly as you!"

Think about what the second man discovered about his friend. His friend was of no use during a time of real difficulty. Think about what your friends discover about you when they're having difficulties. Do they discover that you only worry about yourself? Or do they discover that you're a true friend, one who cares enough to help in times of need?

Prayer

A number of flower seeds (enough for the entire group), a large container of potting mix and a watering can will be needed for this prayer time. Ask the children to sit in a circle on the floor.

Place the gardening items in the centre of the circle.

The prayer begins with a brief quiet time. The instrumental music of ***Happy Are All of My Children*** is quietly played throughout the prayer time.

Leader:

Loving God,
We all experience problems and difficulties in our lives. As a result, we often feel frustrated or angry.
When things go wrong, teach us to look to you for guidance.
We know that disappointment can often turn into opportunity.
Help us to recognise the signs of hope and remain positive when things do not go as we had planned.

Let us be mindful of others who may experience disappointment in their lives and show us how we can reach out to them with love and support. Amen.

Invite each child to select a seed. The children hold the seeds in their hands while they listen to the following prayer.

Leader:

Creator God,
These seeds, like us, and like all of your people, have the potential to grow into beautiful creations. In order for these tiny seeds to reach their full potential they will need to be tended with loving care. They will need to be watered regularly, fed with fertiliser and placed in sunshine where they can draw goodness from the sun's warmth. They will need to be protected against disease and pests, and they will need their leaves and dead flowers pruned from time to time.

Alone they will struggle for life. With the help and care of others, they will grow, and in time become a bouquet of living colour.

Invite the children, one by one, to quietly and prayerfully move forward and plant their seed in the pot of soil. Whist they do so, the leader slowly reads the following scripture verses until all the seeds are planted.

Leader:

Let us listen to the words of Jesus and let our hearts warm to his message of trust, service and love.

Happy are those who are merciful to others,
God will be merciful to them. (Matthew 5: 7)

Happy are those who work for peace,
They will be called God's children. (Matthew 5: 9)

Do for others what you want them to do for you. (Matthew 6: 12)

I was hungry and you fed me,
Thirsty and you gave me a drink,
I was a stranger and you received me in your homes,
Naked and you clothed me,
I was sick and you took care of me,
In prison and you visited me.
I tell you, whenever you did this for the least of these brothers and sisters of mine, you did it for me. (Matthew 25: 35-36, 40)

One of the children is invited to pray the following prayer.

Jesus,
Help us to hear your words, so we can sow seeds of care and love in the lives of others. We thank you that your 'water of life' freely flows on all who are ready and open to receive and welcome it.
Amen.

One of the children waters the seeds and the children are encouraged to listen to the song ***Happy Are All of My Children.***

Song

Happy Are All of My Children

Damien Halloran & Maria Millward

Happy the lost, lonely and poor.
Welcome are you, here at my door.
Happy the meek, gentle and kind.
All that you need, here you will find in me...

Happy the sad, no need to fear.
Come to my arms, comfort is here.
You who would seek justice for all,
Be satisfied - I hear you call to me...

Chorus:
Happy are all of my children
Who walk in the ways of my love.
Come to me,
All that I have is made ready, ready for you.

Happy are you, merciful ones.
Mercy is yours, daughters and sons,
Happy the child pure of heart,
See me and know I'll never part from you...

Chorus
Makers of peace, happy are you.
Children of God in all you do.
Happy when you suffer for right.
I will be there, sharing the night with you...

Chorus

Unit 8

Action

I will ask a parent or carer to tell me about a time when he or she experienced disappointment and how this disappointment was overcome.

Overcoming Fear

Overview

Fear is one of the most powerful emotions we experience, and it can strike quite unexpectedly. We all experience it, regardless of who we are, where we live or what our religious faith might be. However, we do not always experience it in equal measure: the weak and vulnerable tend to experience far more fear than others.

Children are often among the most vulnerable members of any community, and many of them experience a great deal of fear. This unit offers them the chance to explore their experiences of fear and to consider how they might deal with fearful situations.

Outcomes

The children will:

- **recognise that the experience of fearful times and situations is a normal part of every human's journey through life.**
- **identify the people who might best help them cope with their fears.**
- **learn about Jesus' experiences of fearful situations and consider his response.**
- **learn through the teachings of the Bible that God promises to be with them always.**

Unit 9

Getting Started

Fear is one of the most unpleasant emotions we ever feel. It can grip us suddenly and often. We might be walking home from a friend's place after dark. We might see someone we don't know or don't trust - someone we think might hurt us in some way. Perhaps a large, aggressive dog jumps out of the bushes somewhere. Perhaps a parent has had an accident and we don't know if they are going to be all right. Perhaps we have to start at a new school, in a new town or city.

All kinds of things bring fear with them and when we encounter fearful situations, we feel sick and empty, helpless and alone. It is something felt by everyone at times. It is a part of being human. Jesus, for example, felt real fear before he was arrested in Jerusalem.

In the following story, ***The Staircase***, things have gone wrong for a young girl. She is feeling nervous and her fears grow as she climbs an unfamiliar staircase.

Story

The Staircase by John O'Brien

At the front entrance was a long hallway leading to the staircase. It was dark inside, and Marisa held her bag close. She crept quietly forward, frightened that someone might jump from a black shadow and tear it from her.

The air at the base of the staircase was cool and still. It didn't smell nice; it seemed as though someone had been sick there long, long ago. There was a pile of junk half blocking the stairs, too - a couple of rubbish bags, a broken mirror, two mounds of magazines and several old cushions.

Marisa crept up the first flight of stairs. She looked at the two doors on the dingy landing at the top. Did one of them lead into Mrs Compton's flat?

Outside one of the doors there were two small pairs of boots - little kids' boots. Mrs Compton didn't have kids, so it couldn't be her door, but what about the other one? Marisa stepped close. She raised a hand, ready to knock.

But before she did so, she heard a voice from beyond the door. Then another. Loud voices. Angry voices. Arguing about something that had gone missing.

Marisa nervously backed away. She turned and hurried up another flight of stairs, leaving the angry voices behind her.

On the next level was another pair of doors. One was closed, several letters sticking out from underneath it. But the other was open, and Marisa crept closer and peered inside.

"Tara, is that you?" A woman appeared at the far end of a narrow hallway. She had a cigarette in her mouth, and a baby dangled from an arm like a rag doll, like something she had picked up at some stage and forgotten to put down again. She stared at Marisa for a moment. "Have you come for Tara?"

Marisa shook her head.

The woman drew on her cigarette, breathed in, then blew a little cloud of smoke down over the baby. "If you see Tara, you tell her she's in for it when she gets home. Understand?"

"I'm sorry, I don't know Tara," Marisa explained. She smiled nervously. "You see, I've come to stay with..."

"You tell her!" interrupted the woman. "I've had enough of you lot! You come round here for Tara, and if she's in trouble you pretend you don't know her!"

"I really don't..." began Marisa. But then she turned away and raced up the next flight of stairs, not wanting to talk to the woman any more.

There was just a single door the next floor up. Once there had been two, but one of them had been smashed apart. The unit beyond was dark and smelly, and Marisa knew that no one lived there any more.

She stepped up to the one good door, and nervously knocked on it. "Please let it be Mrs Compton's flat," she whispered to herself. "Please let it be."

After a long time, the door slowly squeaked open. A tall man stared down at Marisa. He hadn't shaven in ages, and some of his teeth were missing.

Marisa stepped back, her heart thumping. "I'm sorry," she whispered. "I'm looking for Mrs Compton. I - I thought she might be in there."

"Mrs Compton? In here? Well, maybe she is. Why don't you come in and see." The man laughed, and Marisa could smell alcohol on his breath.

"It's all right." Marisa backed away a little further. Fear twisted through her. She must be upstairs - in her flat. I'll get going now."

The man laughed again, louder than ever. "She might be in here," he said. "In the fridge, maybe. Or under the bed. You come in and have a look."

Unit 9

As he stepped out through the door, Marisa rushed up another flight of stairs. Tears flowed down her cheeks and his horrible laugh echoed behind her.

Her eyes were so blurred she was unable to make out the new doors before her, but when she heard a voice say, "Oh, Marisa. Whatever is the matter?" she almost died with relief.

"Mrs Compton! I'm so glad I've found you!"

Warm fingers wiped away Marisa's tears. A comforting arm slipped around her.

"There, there. Things aren't that bad, dear."

"But, Mrs Compton! When I got home, Mum was gone again. She's gone back to hospital! She left a note telling me to stay with you! But she didn't put the flat number with the address! I didn't know which flat was yours! I didn't know what to do!"

Mrs Compton chuckled. She led Marisa into her flat, hugging her close. "Well, everything's all right now, dear. So don't you worry any more. We'll cook up a lovely dinner - fish and chips, maybe - and I'll make up a nice soft bed on the sofa for you. How does that sound?"

"That sounds great, Mrs Compton. I love fish and chips." Marisa wiped her eyes. She looked all about.

Mrs Compton's flat was small and old. The paint on the walls was faded, the carpet on the floor was threadbare, and some of the windows were cracked.

But the place smelled of flowers and fresh baking, and it felt warm and safe and friendly. Marisa knew she was going to have a wonderful time there. She smiled at Mrs Compton, her fears dissolving away to nothing.

Sharing

The staircase is a new place for Marisa. What are her first impressions of it?

How do you think she feels when she first begins to climb it? Why?

What are some of the things she sees or encounters that add to her fears as she climbs?

What is the most frightening aspect of Marisa's climb? Why is it the most frightening? How does she react to it? Is this a sensible way to react? Why or why not?

Scripture

We can see in Luke's Gospel that Jesus felt real fear the evening he was arrested in Jerusalem. Clearly he knew that dreadful things were about to happen to him.

Read the following scripture passage to the children.

Jesus went out to the Mount of Olives, as he often did, and his disciples went with him. Jesus walked on a little way before he knelt down and prayed, "Father, if you will, please don't make me suffer by having to drink from this cup. But do what you want, and not what I want."

Then an angel from heaven came to help him. Jesus was in great pain, and prayed so sincerely that his sweat fell to the ground like drops of blood. (Luke 22: 41-44)

What did Jesus do when he was afraid? What does he say to his Father? What is God's response. What does this scripture teach us?

During this frightening time, Jesus wanted his friends to keep him company, but they fell asleep, leaving him all alone. When we're alone, our fears can often be stronger. When we are with friendly, caring people, our fears often diminish.

What happens to Marisa's fears at the end of the story? Why does this happen?

Activities

1. Fear Plays

Either have a list of possible settings for the plays on a chart for the group to view, or discuss possible settings with them at the start.

For example:

- school
- street
- hospital/health centre
- park/playground
- beach/pool
- shopping centre
- bush/forest/wood
- friend's house

Ask the children in groups of three or four to make up short plays in which something happens that makes someone frightened. Ask them to develop a realistic situation, taking place at one of the suggested settings. Ask them to show in their play how the frightened person might react to the frightening situation. Share the plays with the group.

After each play, discuss two or three of the following questions.
Was the fearful situation one that really might occur?
What could someone do to avoid similar situations in real life?
How did the frightened person react? What did he/she do?
Are there any other actions that could have been taken?
What could you do if you found yourself in a similar situation?
Who could you go to for help or reassurance?

2. Finding Help

Explain to the children that they are going to consider situations where they've been frightened. To begin the process, it may be helpful for the adult leader to recount briefly a situation where he/she felt frightened and what he/she did to overcome the fear. Afterwards, ask the children to think quietly for a few minutes, and to write briefly about two or three times when they felt frightened.

Invite children to share with the group.

On a large sheet of paper, list situations that the children identified.

For example:

- angry, aggressive dog
- bully at school
- walking from a friend's place after dark

Once the children have finished sharing their experiences, review the list with them and help them identify people who we might have assisted them in these particular situations (e.g. parent, teacher, friend, etc).

To conclude, emphasise the fact that there will always be someone to help us through frightening experiences, and that it is always better to seek help and reassurance than to suffer in silence.

3. Sample Bag of Help

This activity will be done over two sessions.

Tell the children to imagine that they have been employed by the local children's services to put together a sample bag containing helpful and fun items to educate other kids about how to deal with and overcome fear.

Begin with brainstorming all the possible items that could be included in the bag. List these on a sheet of paper.

For example:

- a card detailing the service organisations which exist to help children to deal with their fear
- a stress or worry ball
- a CD of quiet, peaceful music
- a key-ring displaying a positive message such as 'Breathe!'
- a 'happy face' toy

Encourage the children to find or make these items, and any others they think would be helpful, and ask them to bring them to the next session.

When the group meets again, assemble all the items in a central place and one by one ask the 'owner' to explain why he/she would include the item in the bag.

In the future, the contents of the sample bag could be presented by some of the children at a school assembly or a church gathering as an educational tool for the wider community.

4. Body Language

Explain to the children that our bodies often 'tell' us when we are fearful. Explain that many people experience fear, which can in some cases be alleviated if we recognise what is happening in our bodies before we get too worried or wound up.

Sayings such as, 'My legs felt like jelly' and 'I could hardly speak', describe something of how our bodies react to fear.

Ask the children to describe other signs and symptoms of fear which can be expressed by the body.

For example:

- sweaty hands
- shaky legs & hands
- butterflies in the tummy
- increased heart rate
- dry mouth

Encourage the children to become aware of their bodies next time they are confronted by a fearful situation. Tell them that there is a range of helpful things that they can do to help them cope with feelings of fear.

For example:

- slow, deep breathing - in through the nose and out through the mouth
- stretching exercises:

Starting from a crouching position, unfold your body until you are standing on your tip toes with hands reaching out above your head. Hold the position for the count of five and relax.

- singing or making funny noises
- playing quiet, reflective music
- reading a book
- talking to a friend
- talking to God

Choose two or three things from the list and do them with the children.

Reflection

Lonely nights can bring fear: being awake long after midnight, listening to the tap-tap-tapping of a fingerlike branch on a window, the low howl of wind in the trees, and the pitter-patter of hidden paws on the rooftop high above.

Fear can be found in the rush of a crowd, too: being swept away from friends and family, surrounded by hurrying strangers, not knowing where you're going or where you should be.

Fear can strike unexpectedly: coming home to an empty house, with no Mum or Dad, no brothers or sisters, no one there at all.

Fear also comes with change: a new town or city, a new house in a new neighbourhood, a new school, with new teachers and new kids.

What is this feeling that affects us so, tightening our stomach muscles, twisting and turning through our insides, making our hearts thump, our eyes widen, sending shivers rippling through our nervous flesh?

We expect the worst when fear strikes us, but usually the worst doesn't occur. The night sounds die down and we sleep once more. The crowd thins out and we find our way. The delayed family finally gets home. The new place proves friendly.

And even when fear brings real danger, there is usually someone to help with the problem or to talk through the uncertainty. We don't have to let our fears possess us. Though it is not always easy, we can always seek help from someone we trust.

We will all feel fear from time to time, but it is a feeling none of us have to endure alone. We can remember that God is always with us and we can turn to God in prayer at these times.

Prayer

Introduce this prayer by explaining to the children that no matter what their circumstance, God is always with them. Assure them that they are not alone and that if they are feeling anxious or fearful, they can always go to God in prayer.

Remind the children that prayer can take many different forms – formal prayers, praying with God's Word, shared prayer, praying with our bodies using dance and gesture. Tell the children that in this prayer time they are going to be introduced to meditation. Explain that meditation is an ancient, simple prayer form where people become still and quiet in the presence of God.

Ask the children to find a comfortable place to sit or lie. If sitting, they need to make sure that their backs are straight and their feet touch the floor. There should be a reasonable distance between each child.

Leader:

As we prepare for this quiet time of prayer, we listen to God's word, which encourages us not to worry.

'Don't worry about anything, but pray about everything. With thankful hearts offer up your prayers and requests to God. Then, because you belong to Christ Jesus, God will bless you with peace that no one can completely understand. And this peace will control the way you think and feel.' (Phil 4: 6-7)

As we enter into this quiet meditation we become aware that God is with us. We also become aware of our bodies.

We feel the floor or the chair against us.

We become aware of noises – noises inside the room ... and noises outside the room.

Become aware of your breathing – air quietly coming in through your nose and going out through your mouth.

In and out, in and out.

Concentrate on your feet and legs.

Now squeeze your feet and legs for a few seconds and then relax.

Continue to be aware of your breathing.

Now focus on your upper body.

Squeeze your abdomen, take a big breath in and gently exhale.

Continue to be aware of your breathing.

Focus on your arms. Squeeze the muscles in your arms, then release.

Focus now on your neck and face. Tighten all your muscles for a moment and then relax.

You should now feel relaxed and peaceful in the presence of God.

In your heart, speak to Jesus. Tell him that you invite him into this quiet place of prayer. Thank him for the many riches he gives – such as love, friends and people who help us when we are afraid.

Share your thoughts and feelings with Jesus.

(Allow about 1 minute for reflection.)

After you have spent some quiet time in Jesus' presence, gently and quietly become aware of your surroundings. When you are ready, without disturbing anyone else, open your eyes and take a gentle stretch.

Ask the children to sit in a circle. Light a candle to represent Christ and place it in the middle of the group.

Leader:

God who is always with us,

We know you understand all about fear. Jesus your son experienced it when he was on our earth.

Fear is a natural part of being human. We learn to overcome fear when we learn to trust in you.

Thank you for the people who help us when we feel fearful: parents, grandparents, uncles and aunts, and people like teachers, counsellors, ministers, neighbours, doctors and police.

We ask you to give us the strength to help others who may be fearful: a younger child we meet, classmates who may be lonely or uncertain, friends with worrying problems.

When we feel frightened, it is hard to enjoy the gift of life and the many riches you give us. Help us to remember that we are never alone – that you are with us always. Help us to open ourselves to your love, which casts out fear and offers us peace.

Amen.

The children are invited to join in singing ***We Will Make a Place Ready.***

Song

We Will Make a Place Ready

Damien Halloran & Maria Millward

We will make a place ready for you, Jesus.
We will open our arms to your love.
We are happy to sing of the riches you bring.
We will make a place ready in our hearts.

Action

Next time when I am troubled by fear or worry, I will talk to someone I can trust and ask them to help me. I will also ask Jesus to comfort me.

The Promise of New Life

Overview

Death is a topic that many children rarely get the chance to consider and discuss. It is often considered a taboo subject, something to be kept out of sight, something we would rather not think about.

Many children have to confront death, often quite unexpectedly, at a very young age. Children may lose parents, siblings, grand parents or friends through death. Many experience the death of a beloved pet. The sorrow and emptiness that death can bring is well known to a large number of children.

Death, along with the promise of new life, is a part of the essence of Christianity, but many people experiencing death find no glib answers in religion. Faith does not always wash away the pain and sorrow of death. Nor is it meant to. The gospels indicate clearly that Christ was saddened by death, and in fact, feared his own death.

This unit attempts to explore this sensitive issue in a manner accessible to children.

Outcomes

The children will:

- **understand that sadness and grief are natural feelings that people experience when faced with loss and death.**
- **name ways they can support those experiencing the loss of a loved one.**
- **recognise God's promise of new life, clearly expressed through Christ's death and resurrection.**
- **understand that the love and friendship of Jesus is always available to all who are suffering.**

Unit 10

Getting Started

The following story is sad. A girl goes into a classroom to carry out an important but unpleasant task, one she would rather not have to carry out at all.

Her situation is not unusual. Most of us, at some stage in our lives, will experience the unpleasant mix of feelings that she is experiencing. None of us will want to, but life brings sadness along with happiness, and emptiness along with fulfilment.

Story

The Empty Desk by John O'Brien

Anna waits until everyone is gone before she enters the Year Four classroom. She doesn't want anyone to watch her, not even Mrs Garcia.

When the room is quiet and deserted, she slips through the door and gazes nervously at the neat rows of desks filling the room. She recognises Sam's desk at once. None of the others in the room is so jammed with stuff that its lid won't close. None of the others has dozens of bits of paper half-hanging out. None of the others has so much graffiti scribbled all over the top.

One of the desk's hinges is broken, probably because Sam has spent six months trying to force it closed while filled to overflowing. The interior is tightly packed with messy piles of paper, torn exercise books, little broken toys and ancient scraps of food.

Anna steps to the front of the room to collect the rubbish bin. She realises that three-quarters of the stuff in the desk will have to be thrown away, yet she knows that important things are hidden in that desk. She knows she will have to search for them, separating them out from the junk.

She begins to go through the desk with trembling fingers. She throws nothing away thoughtlessly. She gives every bit of scrap paper careful consideration. Many are half-finished pieces of work - spelling, maths, science - and most of these are eventually tossed in the bin. Others are newsletters and other notes that should have made their way home ages ago, and these end up in the bin, too. But a few of the crinkled, untidy pieces of paper in Sam's desk seem important to her, and she piles them carefully on a neighbouring desk.

Some are half-finished stories, messy and unpunctuated, but full of Sam's thoughts and ideas and feelings. Anna chews her lip as she reads these, wishing and wishing she could talk to Sam about them. Some are funny cartoons Sam has been drawing off and on for over a year now. And one is a list of bizarre reasons for not having completed homework. Anna smiles as she quickly glances through it, wondering how many of them Sam has attempted to use during the year.

She keeps most of Sam's exercise books - all except his spelling book. Sam has drawn a series of cartoons on the margins of the pages in this. They're arranged so that when you flip through the pages you see the image of little stick figures involved in violent, bloodthirsty acts. Anna thinks it is rather clever and amusing, but realises it might distress her mother and reluctantly throws it out.

There are quite a few overdue library books in the desk, mostly books by Roald Dahl and J. K. Rowling, Sam's favourite authors. Anna places these on the edge of Mrs Garcia's desk, along with a textbook and a dictionary. She puts the books Sam has defaced at the bottom of the pile, though she is sure Mrs Garcia will not complain about their untidy state.

Near the bottom of the desk, Anna finds a couple of merit awards. The first doesn't surprise her at all; it's for swimming excellence and Sam has always been like a fish in the water. But the second is more puzzling. It has apparently been awarded to Sam for exhibiting mature behaviour while on the class camp early in the year, and Anna can't for a moment imagine her brother exhibiting mature behaviour. Sam has many special qualities, but maturity is certainly not one of them. Her parents have told him to act his age more times than she can remember.

She places the awards on the pile of things she plans to save, wondering why Sam never brought them home. They are the kind of thing that would have thrilled Mum and Dad, and Sam loves thrilling those he cares about. Perhaps he felt embarrassed by them for some reason.

Most of the pens at the bottom of the desk have been broken in half, leaking thick blue ink everywhere. Anna throws these in the bin. She throws out the remains of several ancient food snacks, too. These are mostly dried out, though one retains a healthy crop of fungus. The shards of glass go into the bin, too, along with mounds of pencil sharpenings.

Anna decides to keep some of the toys. Her heart skips a beat as she lifts them out: little plastic monster-men of the kind Sam plays with for hours, a ball of slime like the one he once left in her bed, tiny swords and spears he has carved out of ice cream sticks.

There's not a lot left in the desk now, though the rubbish bin is three-quarters full. The last few scraps of paper she throws away. She pockets the change, and peels off the stickers clinging to the metal base of the desk. And finally it is empty.

Anna places the rubbish bin by the door. Returning to the empty desk, she picks up the pile of things she has decided to save, but finds she is unable to leave the room.

Eyes wide, she stares down at the desk. It seems to reflect exactly the frightening emptiness that developed within her the day an out-of-control car stole her brother's life away.

Finally, she turns and hurries from the Year Four classroom. She holds Sam's things close as she does so. And she hopes they will somehow help to fill her emptiness the way they once helped fill his empty desk to overflowing.

Sharing

Emptying the desk is not easy for Anna - so many of the things in it remind her of her little brother.

What are some of those things and how do they remind her of Sam?

Why might Anna be the one who is emptying the desk, rather than a parent, teacher or classmate?

Why might she have waited until the classroom was deserted before getting started?

What are some of the things we discover about Sam as we see his messy desk through his sister's eyes?

What do you think Anna is going to miss most now that Sam is gone?

What are some of the feelings Anna is experiencing as she goes through Sam's desk? Which of those feelings might we all feel when we lose a loved one?

The next few weeks are not going to be easy for Anna. How might her friends help her during this sad time in her life?

Scripture

Sooner or later, all people experience death and it can be a time of fear, uncertainty, sadness and emptiness. Even Jesus felt these things. He cried when he learned that a friend had died. As he hung upon the cross, near death, he felt more fearful and alone than ever before.

At three o'clock Jesus cried out with a loud shout, "Eloi, Eloi, lema sabachthani?" which means, 'My God, my God, why did you abandon me?' (Mark 15:34)

Yet, moments before his death, he expressed trust and hope that God would protect him.

Jesus cried out in a loud voice, "Father, in your hands I place my spirit." He said this and died. (Luke 23:46)

In many ways, Jesus reacted to death the way most people do. Yet, almost at the moment of his death, we can see in his words a hint of the new life God has promised to us all.

Activities

1. Loss

Discuss with the group the many losses that can affect us: the loss of a parent or grandparent, a brother or sister, some other relative, a friend, neighbour or even a loved pet. Briefly consider the many ways we can experience loss (e.g. family break-up, moving house, sickness, going to a different school, etc).

Ask the children to consider some of the losses they've experienced. Ask them to select one instance of loss. Give them modelling clay and ask them to create a sculpture which in some way represents the feelings they had at this time of loss.

Once they have finished, ask for volunteers to show and discuss their sculptures with the group.

2 Life Cycle

Explain to the group that all living things experience a life cycle that will end with physical death. Discuss some examples (e.g. the life cycle of a butterfly).

Discuss how humans, too, grow and change as they live through different stages in their lives (e.g. baby, child, teenager, adult and old age).

Ask the children to draw a series of little pictures illustrating the stages in the life of a person (or a series of symbols representing those stages) beginning with birth and ending with death.

Afterwards, have them present their work to the group, explaining what their various pictures or symbols represent. Point out to the children that as followers of Jesus, we believe in new life after physical death.

3. The Death of Jesus

Explain to the group that the friends of Jesus were fearful, anxious and horrified by what happened to him in Jerusalem. They grieved terribly at his death, but when they met him after his resurrection, they were filled with new hope.

In pairs, have the children illustrate key events relating to the death of Jesus. Ask them to include some friends of Jesus in their illustrations. Encourage the children to use the Bible as a point of reference.

Examples might be:

- carrying the cross
- being crucified
- dying on the cross
- being buried
- meeting with his friends after the resurrection

Afterwards, have them present their illustrations to the group, explaining how they think the friends of Jesus might have felt while witnessing these incidents.

4. Helping a Friend

Have the children, in pairs or small groups, draw up lists of things they could do to help or comfort a grieving friend who has suffered the loss of a loved one. (It might be useful to discuss briefly some possible examples with the whole group first.)

Ask them to decide which two or three things on their lists would be most helpful to the friend and why.

Afterwards, have them report back to the whole group and discuss the results.

Reflection

Death will affect us all during our lives. We will lose people we care about, sometimes slowly, sometimes quickly, and sometimes without any warning at all. This will leave us with an emptiness that may take a long, long time to fill.

Jesus knew well the sadness of death, the sadness of finding that a loved one was walking this earth no more. He shed tears, like any loving human, for friends who had died. He knew the sadness and emptiness of loss. But Jesus also knew the promise of his father, the promise of new life.

He expressed his trust in his father at the moment of his death, despite his pain and suffering. He knew he would soon be sheltering in his father's arms.

We know that the death of a loved one brings sadness and pain. Like Jesus, we will put our trust in God, knowing that new life is something God has promised to all of his children.

Prayer

During this prayer time the children will make a butterfly.
(See illustration below.)

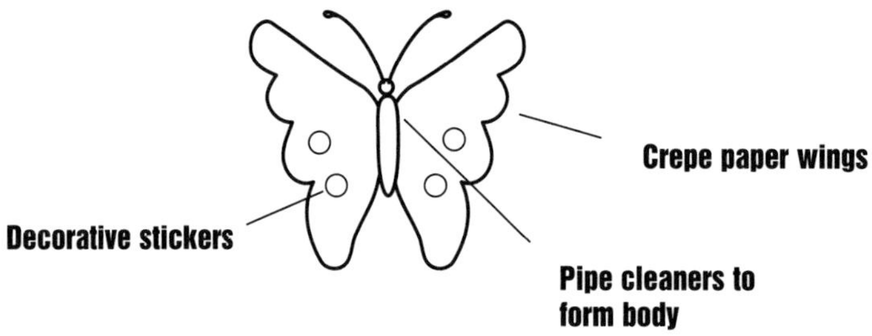

A number of craft items will be needed. It would be helpful for the leader to demonstrate how to make the butterfly before commencing the prayer.

Seat the children in a circle. In the middle, place pipe cleaners, scissors, colourful decorating stickers and lengths of crepe paper, enough for each child. Tell the children that they will be asked to make a butterfly using the craft items.

Suggest to the children that while they are making their butterflies they should think about a special person whom they may have lost through death or separation (or any other loss) and that their butterfly will symbolise the life of that person. Some children may not have themselves experienced loss as described. Suggest that they could think of someone else, such as a friend or relative who has experienced loss, and offer the prayer for them.

Tell the children that this exercise will be done in a prayerful, reflective atmosphere.

Invite the children to listen carefully to the following Bible reading.

I am certain that nothing can separate us from God's love: neither death, nor life, neither angel nor other heavenly rulers or powers, neither the present nor the future, neither the world above nor the world below - there is nothing in all creation that will ever be able to separate us from the love of God which is ours through Christ Jesus our Lord.

(Romans 8: 39)

The following prayer is read by one of the children.

Jesus,
When we experience loss in our lives we feel many different emotions: sadness, anger, frustration, fear...We know that these feelings are natural. Help us to have the courage to seek out others who can help us deal with our loss. We thank you that you are always with us and that you always listen to us. Help us to take all our sadness to you. Bless us, and all people who may be troubled or worried at this time.
Amen.

Ask the children to come forward one by one and take the craft items they will need to make their butterflies.

Reflective music is played while the children are creating their butterflies.

After they finish making their butterflies, the leader, or one of the children, leads the following prayer, and the others respond.

Leader:
God our Creator, we thank you for the precious gift of life.

All:
Thank you for the gift of life.

Leader:
God our Creator, we thank you for the people in our lives who love us and care for us.

All:
Thank you for the gift of life.

Leader:
God our Creator, we thank you for the gift of the lives of the people our butterflies represent. For the love, the laughter and the memories, we give you thanks.

All:

Thank you for the gift of life. Teach us how to give you our sadness and open our hearts to your love. Let us see that nothing can take us away from your love.

After the prayer, the children are invited to take their butterflies home as a symbol of new life.

Explain to the children that some people in the group may be feeling sad due to a death or a loss in their lives. Remind the children that sad feelings are a natural and an important part of growing through the difficult times. Tell the children that there is no need for them to feel alone at this time, that there are people who are experienced in helping children who are are sad. Tell the children that you can arrange a time for them to talk with one of these people, if they wish.

The song, ***Nothing Can Take Us Away,*** is played to conclude the prayer. The children are invited to join in the singing, if they wish.

Song

Nothing Can Take Us Away

Damien Halloran & Maria Millward

We are certain that nothing
Can take us away from your love.
Not death, nor life,
No power below or above.
There is nothing present or past
And nothing to come,
To keep us from knowing the love
Of Jesus, your son.

Chorus:
Hold us now,
Teach us how
To give you our sadness and open our hearts to your love.
Set us free,
Let us see
That nothing can take us away, away from your love.

We are never alone,
Even though we're in sorrow and pain.
You come to us,
You're making us happy again.
You're the light in darkness,
You shine in ev'ry new day,
A friend to the lonely,
The one to show us the way.

Chorus

Action

If I am ever worried or troubled about death or any other form of loss, I will talk to a caring adult about how I am feeling.

When We Listen

Words: Maria Millward

Music: Damien Halloran
Arr. David Pudney

CHORUS:
G D A7 Bm G
When we listen, we will hear you— speak - ing to us—
D D/F♯ Em7 G6 Asus4 A Gadd9 D
of your won - der - ful ways. When we lis - ten,—
F♯7 Bm G A D G/D D G/D
we will hear you,— guid - ing us all of our days.
1, 2.
G/A A/C♯
When we
3.
Bm A G D/F♯ Em A7 D
days— Guid - ing us all of our days.

We've Got The Power

Words: Maria Millward

Music: Damien Halloran
Arr. Jared Haschek

Gmaj7 A D A/D
po - wer. We've got the free - dom to choose. We've got the po -
Gmaj7 A D A/D
- wer. You know, we can - not lose! We've got the pow -
Gmaj7 A Bm7 A/B
- wer. Hey, have you heard the news? We've got the
Em7 D/F♯ Asus A
free - dom and the po - wer to choose, the po - wer to choose.

Em7
D/F♯
Asus
And if we want to we can make this day a bet - ter day.
(We have the free - dom,
A
Em7
D/F♯
And if we want to we can show this world a bet - ter way!
we have the po - wer to - day!)
Gadd2
A
B
We've got the
(What do you say?)
Amaj7
B
E
B/E
po - wer. We've got the free - dom to choose. We've got the po -

Amaj7
B
E
B/E
- wer. You know, we can - not lose! We've got the po -
Amaj7
B
C♯m7
B/C♯
- wer. Hey, have you heard the news? We've got the
F♯m7
E/G♯
1.
Bsus
B
2.
Bsus
B
E
free - dom and the po - wer to choose, We've got the the po - wer to choose.

Good Things

Words: Maria Millward

Music: Damien Halloran and Maria Millward
Arr. Jared Haschek

VERSES:
F/G C F/G C F C/E Dm C
good things!"
(send good things)
1. God is glad to have made us. Oh, so glad
2. God is glad to be with us. Oh, so glad
D7 D7/C Gsus G
1.
Dm7 C/E F G
to have made us. Ma - ny gifts God sends us ev - 'ry day! Ev - 'ry day those
to be with us. God is al - ways list - 'ning when we pray. Ev - 'ry day those
1.
2.
Asus A
CHORUS:
D
Good things are com - ing our way
(good things) (are com - ing our way) —
2.

Em G/A A G/A A
Good things God sends us to - day! God says,
(good things)
G D A A♯dim7 Bm E7 E7/G♯
"What should I send— to all of my friends? I'll send
D/A G/A D G/A D
2nd time to Coda
good things! I'll send good things!"
(send good things) (send good things)
2nd time to Coda
G D/F♯ Em D
Praise our God for the good things. Thank our God for the good things,

E7
E7/D
Asus A
Em7 D/F♯ G A
D.S al Coda
cel - e - brate the gifts God sends to - day!
Ev - 'ry day those
D.S al Coda
CODA:
D/A
G/A D
"I'll send good things! I'll send good things!"
(good things) (send good things)

We Will Bring Your Peace

Words: Maria Millward

Music: Damien Halloran

Em G/A A7 G/A D
Je - sus, you ask us to be kind,
Je - sus, you ask us to be fair,
Bm F♯m/A E
to take good care of each o - ther, then your
to take good care of each o - ther, then your
Em G F♯m Em7 G/B Asus4 A7 G/B
D.S al Fine
peace will be here for all to find. We will
peace will be here for all to share. We will
D.S al Fine

I Will Bless You, Lord

Lyrics: Maria Millward

Music: Damien Halloran
Piano Arr. Tim Hildebrandt

Dm G7 C Fmaj7
Our health and hap - pi - ness you send. You're al - ways rea - dy to for -
You are our strength when we are weak and e - ver safe with - in your
Em7 Dm7 G
REFRAIN:
- give. Your pa - tient love will ne - ver end. I will
sight. Your ten - der love is what we seek.
C Am Dm
bless you, Lord, with all my heart. I will bless your ho - ly
G Am Em
name! You are a lov - ving God, a for - giv - ing God, I will

1.
2.
Dm G C C A♭7
bless your ho - ly name! name! I will
D♭ B♭m E♭m
bless you, Lord, with all my heart. I will bless your ho - ly
A♭ B♭m Fm
name! You are a lo - ving God, a for - giv - ing God. I will
E♭m A♭ D♭ B♭m
bless your ho - ly name! You are a lo - ving God, a for -

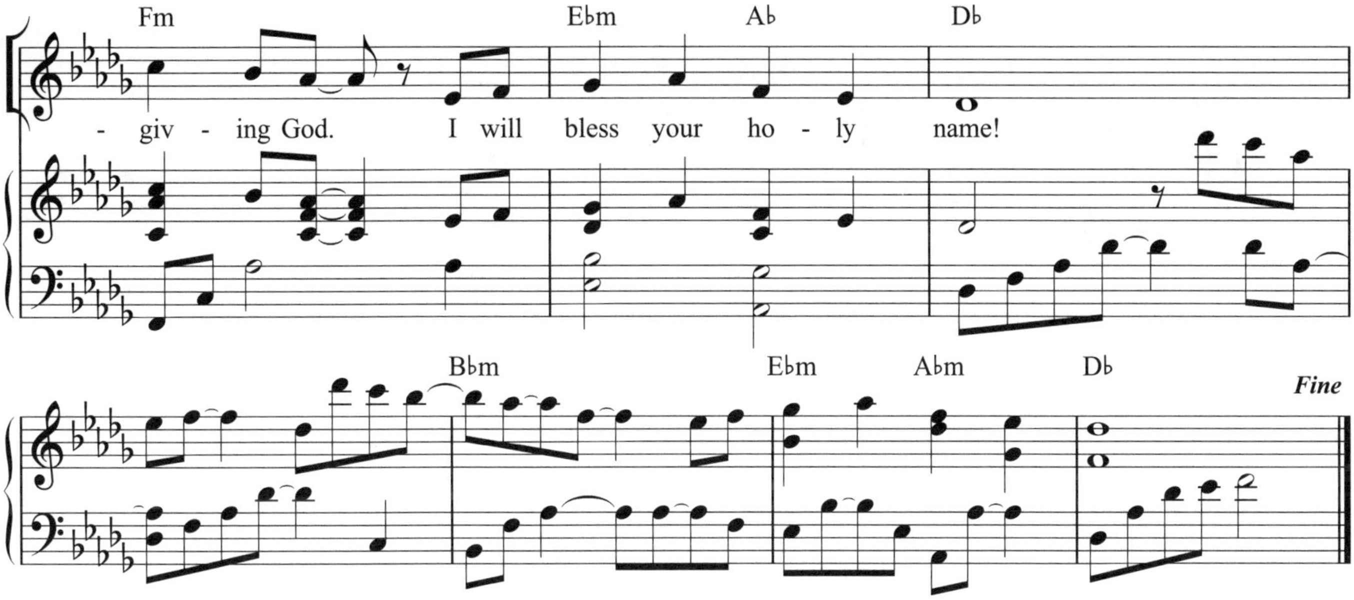
Fm
Ebm
Ab
Db
- giv - ing God. I will bless your ho - ly name!
Bbm
Ebm
Abm
Db
Fine

Welcome To God's House

Words: Maria Millward

Music: Damien Halloran

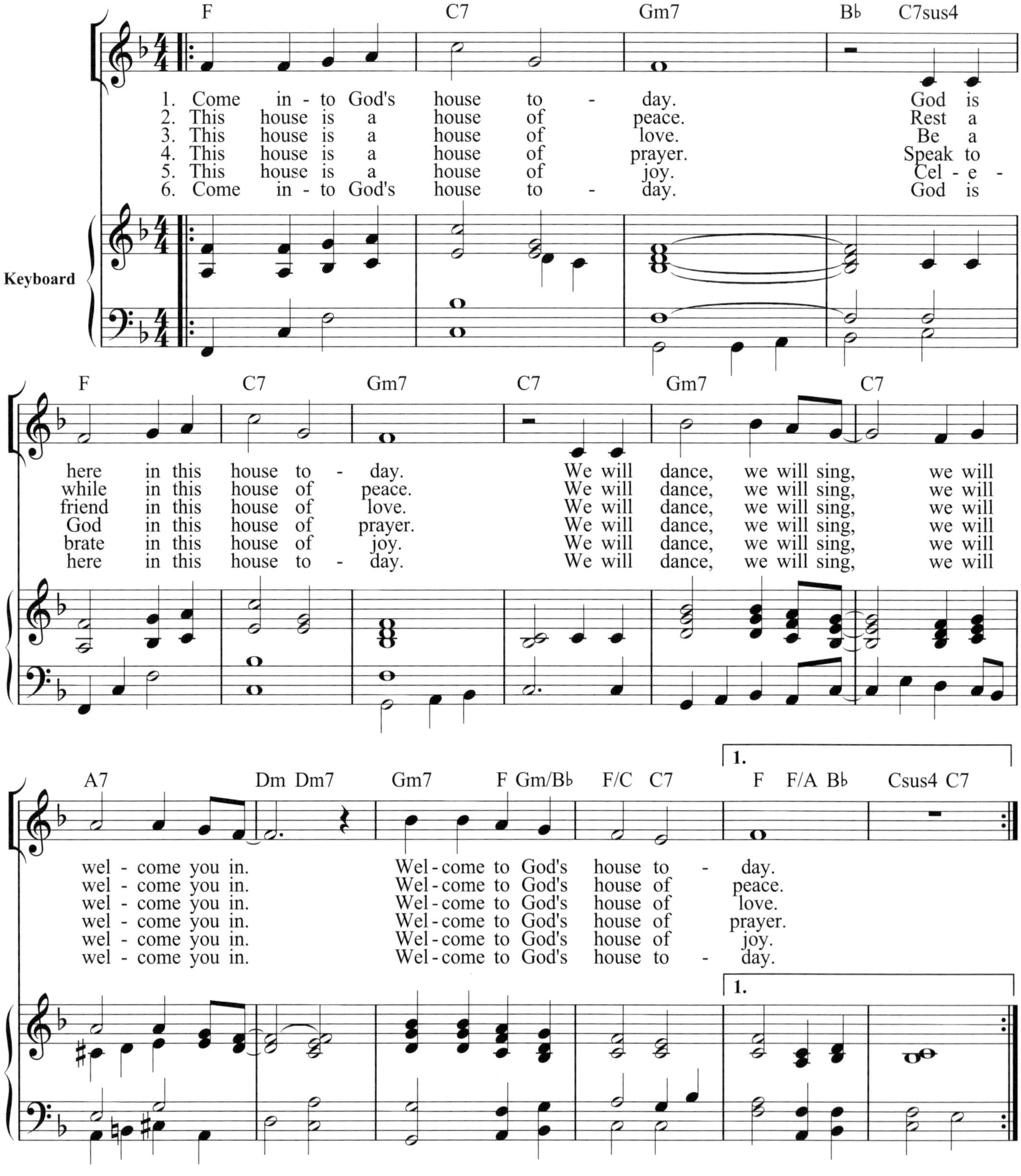

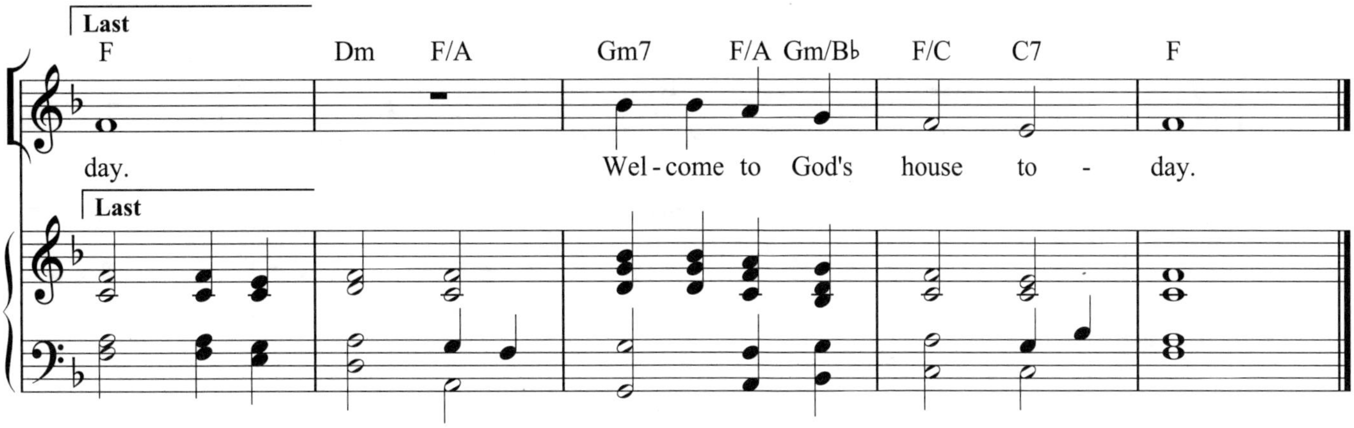
Last
F Dm F/A Gm7 F/A Gm/B♭ F/C C7 F
day. Wel - come to God's house to - day.
Last

Do To Others

Words: Maria Millward

Music: Damien Halloran

2.
B♭ F F7 B♭
1. Diff - 'rent eyes we have to see, and
2. diff - 'rent gifts we have to share, to
Dm G9
diff - 'rent points of view, with diff - 'rent hopes and diff - 'rent dreams — for
help each o - ther see that all of us must learn to care for
CODA:
B♭/C C F Dm7
D.C al Coda 2nd time
you and me, for me and you. And
each one in God's fam - i - ly.
Gm7 B♭/C F B♭ F
Do to o - thers as you would have them do to you.

Happy Are All Of My Children

Words: Maria Millward

Music: Damien Halloran
Arr. Jared Haschek

Amaj7 Bm/A A D/A Amaj7
gen - tle and kind. All that you need here you will
jus - tice for all, be sat - is - fied; I hear you
Bm/A A D/A A
find in me.
call to me.
CHORUS:
E/G♯ A E/G♯
Hap - py are all of my chil - dren, who walk in the ways of my
F♯m E/G♯ E F♯m E D
love. Come to me, all that I have is made rea - dy,

D/E
A
D/A
A
3rd time to Coda
rea - dy for you.
3rd time to Coda
VERSES 3, 4:
Bm7
A/C♯
D
Hap - py are you, mer - ci - ful ones.
Ma - kers of peace, hap - py are you,
A
Bm7
A/C♯
D
Mer - cy is yours, daugh - ters and sons.
chil - dren of God in all you do.
A
Bm7
A/C♯
D
Hap - py the child pure of heart.
Hap - py when you suf - fer for right.

A
Bm7
A/C♯
D
See me and know I'll ne - ver part from
I will be there, sha - ring the night with
A
D/A
A
D.S al Coda
you.
you.
D.S al Coda
CODA:
A
Bm7
A/C♯
D
A
you.
Play four times

We Will Make A Place Ready

Words: Maria Millward

Music: Damien Halloran
Arr. David Pudney

1.
Em7
Am7
Dm7
G7
a place is
make a place rea - dy in our hearts. We will
1.
2.
G7
C
Fm
C
in our hearts.
2.
Fm6
C

Nothing Can Take Us Away

Words: Maria Millward

Music: Damien Halloran
Arr. David Pudney

Em7 A7 D G/A D
keep us from know - ing the love of Je - sus, your son.
friend to the lone - ly, the one to show us the way.
keep us from know - ing the love of Je - sus, your son.
CHORUS:
A7 Bm F♯m7 G Em7 D/F♯
Hold us now, teach us how to give you our sad - ness and o - pen our hearts to your
G6 A A/C♯ A7 Bm F♯m G
love. Set us free, let us see that

1, 2.
Em7 G6 A7 D G/A D
no - thing can take us a - way, a - way from your love. We are
1, 2.
3.
Bm G F♯m7 Em7 G6
love. No - thing can take us a -
3.
A7 D G/A D
- way, a - way from your love.

When We Listen

Damien Halloran & Maria Millward

1. When we listen, we will hear you,
In the towering voices of mountains
and seas.
When we listen, we will hear you,
In the gentlest song of the breeze.

Refrain:

When we listen, we will hear you,
Speaking to us of your wonderful ways.
When we listen, we will hear you,
Guiding us all of our days.

2. When we listen we will hear you,
In the welcoming warmth of our fam'ly
and friends.
When we listen, we will hear you,
In the laughter and love that you send.

Refrain:

When we listen, we will hear you,
Speaking to us of your wonderful ways.
When we listen, we will hear you,
Guiding us all of our days.

3. When we listen, we will hear you,
In the stories and songs that your
people have heard.
When we listen, we will hear you,
In the power of your holy word.

We’ve Got the Power

Damien Halloran & Maria Millward

1. You give us courage
For each choice we make,
Strength along each road we take,
Help to learn from each mistake.
But we’ve got the power,
(the power to choose),
We’ve got the power!

Chorus:

We’ve got the power,
We’ve got the freedom to choose.
We’ve got the power,
You know we cannot lose!
We’ve got the power,
Hey, have you heard the news?
We’ve got the freedom and the power to choose,
The power to choose!

2. You give us fam’ly,
And good friends to know,
Love and laughter as we go,
Time to wonder, room to grow,
But we’ve got the power,
(the power to choose),
We’ve got the power!

Chorus:

We’ve got the power,
We’ve got the freedom to choose.
We’ve got the power,
You know we cannot lose!
We’ve got the power,
Hey, have you heard the news?
We’ve got the freedom and the power to choose,
The power to choose!

Repeat Chorus

Bridge:

And if we want to we can make this day a better day!
(We have the freedom, we have the power today!)
And if we want to we can show this world a better way!
(What do you say?)

Chorus:

We've got the power,
We've got the freedom to choose.
We've got the power,
You know we cannot lose!
We've got the power,
Hey, have you heard the news?
We've got the freedom and the power to choose,
The power to choose!

Repeat Chorus

Good Things

Damien Halloran & Maria Millward

Chorus:

Good things (good things),
Are coming our way (are coming our way).
Good things (good things),
God sends us today!
God says, "What shall I send to all of my friends?
I'll send good things (send good things),
I'll send good things (send good things)!"

1. God is glad to have made us,
Oh, so glad to have made us.
Many gifts God sends us every day.
Every day those...

Chorus:

2. God is glad to be with us,
Oh, so glad to be with us.
God is always listening when we pray.
Every day those...

Chorus:

3. Praise our God for the good things,
Thank our God for the good things,
Celebrate the gifts God sends today!
Every day those...

Chorus:

Good things (good things),
Are coming our way (are coming our way).
Good things (good things),
God sends us today!
God says, "What shall I send to all of my friends?
I'll send good things (send good things),
I'll send good things (send good things)!"

We Will Bring Your Peace

Damien Halloran & Maria Millward

Refrain:

We will bring your peace into the world.
We will bring your peace into the world.
With a loving hand, do the best we can;
We will bring your peace to the world. (x2)

1. Jesus you ask us to be gentle,
Jesus you ask us to be kind,
To take good care of each other,
Then your peace will be here for all to find.

Refrain:

2. Jesus you ask us to be friendly,
Jesus you ask us to be fair,
To take good care of each other,
Then your peace will be here for all to share.

Refrain:

I Will Bless You, Lord

Damien Halloran & Maria Millward

Refrain:

I will bless you, Lord, with all my heart.
I will bless your holy name!
You are a loving God, a forgiving God.
I will bless your holy name!

1. You give us all we need to live;
Our health and happiness you send.
You're always ready to forgive;
Your patient love will never end.

Refrain:

2. You help us work for what is right.
You are our strength when we are weak,
And ever safe within your sight,
Your tender love is what we seek.

Refrain:

Welcome to God's House

Damien Halloran & Maria Millward

1. Come into God's house today.
God is here in this house today.
We will dance, we will sing,
We will welcome you in!
Welcome to God's house today!

2. This house is a house of peace.
Rest awhile in this house of peace.
We will dance, we will sing,
We will welcome you in!
Welcome to God's house of peace!

3. This house is a house of love.
Be a friend in this house of love.
We will dance, we will sing,
We will welcome you in!
Welcome to God's house of love!

4. This house is a house of prayer.
Speak to God in this house of prayer.
We will dance, we will sing,
We will welcome you in!
Welcome to God's house of prayer!

5. This house is a house of joy.
Celebrate in this house of joy.
We will dance, we will sing,
We will welcome you in!
Welcome to God's house of joy!

6. Come into God's house today,
God is here in this house today,
We will dance, we will sing,
We will welcome you in!
Welcome to God's house today!

Do to Others

Damien Halloran & Maria Millward

1. Do to others as you would have them do
   to you.
   Say to others as you would have them
   say to you.
   Think before you speak and act,
   We're all God's children – that's a fact, so
   Do to others as you would have them do
   to you.

2. Do to others as you would have them do
   to you.
   Say to others as you would have them
   say to you.
   Walk a while in others' shoes,
   It's easy then to always choose to
   Do to others as you would have them do
   to you.

Bridge:

Different eyes we have to see,
And different points of view,
With different hopes and different dreams:
For you and me, for me and you, and
Different gifts we have to share,
To help each other see
That all of us must learn to care
For each one in God's family, and

3. Do to others as you would have them do
 to you.
 Say to others as you would have them
 say to you.
 Think before you speak and act,
 We're all God's children – that's a fact, so
 Do to others as you would have them do
 to you.

Happy Are All of My Children

Damien Halloran & Maria Millward

1. Happy the lost, lonely and poor.
   Welcome are you, here at my door.
   Happy the meek, gentle and kind.
   All that you need, here you will
      find in me.

2. Happy the sad, no need to fear.
   Come to my arms, comfort is here.
   You who would seek justice for all,
   Be satisfied – I hear you call to me.

Chorus:

Happy are all of my children
Who walk in the ways of my love.
Come to me,
All that I have is made ready,
Ready for you.

3. Happy are you, merciful ones.
Mercy is yours, daughters and
sons.
Happy the child, pure of heart.
See me and know I'll never part
from you.

Chorus:

Happy are all of my children
Who walk in the ways of my love.
Come to me,
All that I have is made ready,
Ready for you.

4. Makers of peace, happy are you,
Children of God in all you do.
Happy when you suffer for right,
I will be there, sharing the night
with you.

Chorus:

Nothing Can Take Us Away

Damien Halloran & Maria Millward

1. We are certain that nothing
   can take us away from your love.
   Not death, nor life,
   No power below or above.
   There is nothing present or past
   and nothing to come,
   To keep us from knowing the love
   of Jesus, your son.

Refrain:

Hold us now,
Teach us how
To give you our sadness and open
our hearts to your love.
Set us free,
Let us see
That nothing can take us away,
away from your love.

2. We are never alone
Even through we're in sorrow and pain.
You come to us,
You're making us happy again.
You're the light in darkness,
You shine in ev'ry new day,
A friend to the lonely,
The one to show us the way.

Refrain:

Hold us now,
Teach us how
To give you our sadness and open
our hearts to your love.
Set us free,
Let us see
That nothing can take us away,
away from your love.
Nothing can take us away,
away from your love.